GVSTAV KLIMT

2000 DIARY

evergreen

Gustav Klimt (1862–1918)

The Vienna of the Belle Epoque – of Sigmund Freud, Mahler and Schönberg – has prompted the admiration of the whole world for the quality and diversity of its cultural and artistic life. And Gustav Klimt (1862–1918) was without doubt its defining and most fascinating painter.

As a highly gifted student he decorated the walls of the Burgtheater, the staircase of the Art History Museum, the University of Vienna and the Stoclet Palace. As an art revolutionary he headed the Secession of 1897, reacting against the official academic world and bourgeois conservatism.

Cloaked in richly woven patterns of gold or silver, in mosaics, exotic designs, fairy-tale illustrations of birds and animals, ornamental or floral motifs, mystical whirls or kaleidoscopes of radiant colours, Klimt's seductive portrayals of nudity reach down into the secrets of the unconscious and the labyrinths of the mind. He confronted the public with his own unwavering sensuality and the omnipresence of Eros in the workings of the world, creating the true erotic prelude to modern sexuality – of which Expressionism and Surrealism were to make such arresting use.

Das Wien der Belle Epoque – die Stadt Sigmund Freuds und Otto Wagners, Mahlers und Schönbergs – wird in der ganzen Welt bewundert wegen der Qualität und Vielfalt seines kulturellen und künstlerischen Lebens. Und Gustav Klimt (1862–1918) ist ohne Zweifel sein repräsentativster und faszinierendster Maler.

Als hervorragend begabter Schüler hat er die Wände des Burgtheaters, das Treppenhaus des Kunsthistorischen Museums, die Wiener Universität und das Palais Stoclet ausgestattet. Als Revolutionär stand er an der Spitze der Secession von 1897, die gegen den offiziellen Akademismus und den bürgerlichen Konservatismus opponierte.

Unter einem Mantel von Gold und Silber, Mosaiken, Exotismen, einem märchenhaften Bestiarium von Vögeln und Tieren, Blumenmotiven und Ornamenten, von mystischen Wirbeln oder grellfarbigen Kaleidoskopen entführt der Maler seine aggressiven Nacktheiten zu den Geheimnissen des Unbewußten und den Labyrinthen des Geistes und bringt uns so seine unbeirrbare Sinnlichkeit nahe und die Allgegenwart des Eros im Kreislauf der Welt. Auf diese Weise schafft er ein erotisches Präludium für die moderne Sexualität, von der Expressionismus und Surrealismus so beharrlich Gebrauch machen werden.

Klimt in Painter's Smock, with Cat | Klimt mit Malerkittel und Katze vor seinem Atelier
Klimt et son chat devant l'atelier | Klimt con bata de pintor y sosteniendo un gato

Gustav Klimt (1862–1918)

La Vienne de la Belle Epoque – celle de Sigmund Freud et d'Otto Wagner, de Mahler et de Schönberg – suscite l'admiration du monde entier pour la qualité et la diversité de sa vie culturelle et artistique. Et Gustav Klimt (1862–1918) en est sans conteste le peintre le plus représentatif et le plus fascinant.

Elève surdoué, il a décoré les murs du Burgtheater, l'escalier du Kunsthistorisches Museum, l'Université de Vienne, le palais Stoclet. Révolutionnaire, il a pris la tête de la Sécession de 1897, destinée à réagir contre l'académisme officiel et le conservatisme bourgeois.

Sous couvert d'or et d'argent, de mosaïques, d'exotisme, de fabuleux bestiaires d'oiseaux et d'animaux, de motifs floraux ou ornementaux, de tourbillons mystiques ou de kaléidoscopes aux couleurs ardentes, c'est vers les arcanes de l'inconscient et les labyrinthes de l'esprit que le peintre entraîne ses nudités agressives, traduisant ainsi son inaliénable sensualité et l'omniprésence d'Eros à travers le cycle du monde. Ce faisant, il constitue par là même le véritable prélude érotique à la sexualité moderne dont l'Expressionnisme et le Surréalisme feront un si constant usage.

Het Wenen van 'la Belle Epoque' –van Sigmund Freud, Otto Wagner, Mahler en Schönberg– wekt de bewondering van de hele wereld om de kwaliteit en verscheidenheid van zijn culturele en artistieke leven. En Gustav Klimt (1862–1918) is zonder meer de boeiendste en representatiefste schilder uit die periode.

Als buitengewoon begaafd leerling beschilderde hij de muren van het Burgtheater, de trap van het Kunsthistorisches Museum, de universiteit van Wenen en het paleis Stoclet. Hij was revolutionair en nam dan ook de leiding in de Sezession van 1897, bedoeld als protest tegen het officiële academisme en het burgerlijke conservatisme.

Klimt schildert agressieve naakten, die hij vormgeeft met zilver en goud, mozaïeken, exotisme, fabelachtige bestiaria van vogels en dieren, sier- en bloemmotieven, mystieke wervelingen of vurig gekleurde caleidoscopen. Hij voert deze vrouwen mee naar de geheimen van het onderbewuste en de labyrinten van de geest en geeft zo de onvervreemdbare sensualiteit en de alomtegenwoordigheid van Eros in de cyclus van het heelal weer. Hij kan worden beschouwd als de wegbereider van de moderne seksualiteit van het Expressionisme en het Surrealisme.

Klimt's Studio | Klimts Atelier
L'atelier de Klimt | El estudio de Klimt

Klimt and Emilie Flöge in a Dress Designed by Klimt | Klimt und Emilie Flöge in einem von Klimt entworfenen Kleid
Klimt et Emilie Flöge dans une robe dessinée par Klimt | Klimt y Emilie Flöge con un vestido diseñado por Klimt
1918. *Österreichische NationalBibliothek* / © *Photo: Bildarchiv / ÖNB, Wien*

Year Planner | Jahresplaner | Planning | Planning **1999**

September		October		November		December	
1 We		1 Fr		1 Mo	44	1 We	
2 Th		2 Sa		2 Tu		2 Th	
3 Fr		3 Su		3 We		3 Fr	
4 Sa		4 Mo	40	4 Th		4 Sa	
5 Su		5 Tu		5 Fr		5 Su	
6 Mo	36	6 We		6 Sa		6 Mo	49
7 Tu		7 Th		7 Su		7 Tu	
8 We		8 Fr		8 Mo	45	8 We	
9 Th		9 Sa		9 Tu		9 Th	
10 Fr		10 Su		10 We		10 Fr	
11 Sa		11 Mo	41	11 Th		11 Sa	
12 Su		12 Tu		12 Fr		12 Su	
13 Mo	37	13 We		13 Sa		13 Mo	50
14 Tu		14 Th		14 Su		14 Tu	
15 We		15 Fr		15 Mo	46	15 We	
16 Th		16 Sa		16 Tu		16 Th	
17 Fr		17 Su		17 We		17 Fr	
18 Sa		18 Mo	42	18 Th		18 Sa	
19 Su		19 Tu		19 Fr		19 Su	
20 Mo	38	20 We		20 Sa		20 Mo	51
21 Tu		21 Th		21 Su		21 Tu	
22 We		22 Fr		22 Mo	47	22 We	
23 Th		23 Sa		23 Tu		23 Th	
24 Fr		24 Su		24 We		24 Fr	
25 Sa		25 Mo	43	25 Th		25 Sa	
26 Su		26 Tu		26 Fr		26 Su	
27 Mo	39	27 We		27 Sa		27 Mo	52
28 Tu		28 Th		28 Su		28 Tu	
29 We		29 Fr		29 Mo	48	29 We	
30 Th		30 Sa		30 Tu		30 Th	
		31 Su				31 Fr	

Year Planner | Jahresplaner | Planning | Planning **2000**

January				February				March				April		
1	Sa			1	Tu			1	We			1	Sa	
2	Su			2	We			2	Th			2	Su	
3	Mo	1		3	Th			3	Fr			3	Mo	14
4	Tu			4	Fr			4	Sa			4	Tu	
5	We			5	Sa			5	Su			5	We	
6	Th			6	Su			6	Mo	10		6	Th	
7	Fr			7	Mo	6		7	Tu			7	Fr	
8	Sa			8	Tu			8	We			8	Sa	
9	Su			9	We			9	Th			9	Su	
10	Mo	2		10	Th			10	Fr			10	Mo	15
11	Tu			11	Fr			11	Sa			11	Tu	
12	We			12	Sa			12	Su			12	We	
13	Th			13	Su			13	Mo	11		13	Th	
14	Fr			14	Mo	7		14	Tu			14	Fr	
15	Sa			15	Tu			15	We			15	Sa	
16	Su			16	We			16	Th			16	Su	
17	Mo	3		17	Th			17	Fr			17	Mo	16
18	Tu			18	Fr			18	Sa			18	Tu	
19	We			19	Sa			19	Su			19	We	
20	Th			20	Su			20	Mo	12		20	Th	
21	Fr			21	Mo	8		21	Tu			21	Fr	
22	Sa			22	Tu			22	We			22	Sa	
23	Su			23	We			23	Th			23	Su	
24	Mo	4		24	Th			24	Fr			24	Mo	17
25	Tu			25	Fr			25	Sa			25	Tu	
26	We			26	Sa			26	Su			26	We	
27	Th			27	Su			27	Mo	13		27	Th	
28	Fr			28	Mo	9		28	Tu			28	Fr	
29	Sa			29	Tu			29	We			29	Sa	
30	Su							30	Th			30	Su	
31	Mo	5						31	Fr					

Year Planner | Jahresplaner | Planning | Planning **2000**

May			June			July			August		
1	Mo	18	1	Th		1	Sa		1	Tu	
2	Tu		2	Fr		2	Su		2	We	
3	We		3	Sa		3	Mo	27	3	Th	
4	Th		4	Su		4	Tu		4	Fr	
5	Fr		5	Mo	23	5	We		5	Sa	
6	Sa		6	Tu		6	Th		6	Su	
7	Su		7	We		7	Fr		7	Mo	32
8	Mo	19	8	Th		8	Sa		8	Tu	
9	Tu		9	Fr		9	Su		9	We	
10	We		10	Sa		10	Mo	28	10	Th	
11	Th		11	Su		11	Tu		11	Fr	
12	Fr		12	Mo	24	12	We		12	Sa	
13	Sa		13	Tu		13	Th		13	Su	
14	Su		14	We		14	Fr		14	Mo	33
15	Mo	20	15	Th		15	Sa		15	Tu	
16	Tu		16	Fr		16	Su		16	We	
17	We		17	Sa		17	Mo	29	17	Th	
18	Th		18	Su		18	Tu		18	Fr	
19	Fr		19	Mo	25	19	We		19	Sa	
20	Sa		20	Tu		20	Th		20	Su	
21	Su		21	We		21	Fr		21	Mo	34
22	Mo	21	22	Th		22	Sa		22	Tu	
23	Tu		23	Fr		23	Su		23	We	
24	We		24	Sa		24	Mo	30	24	Th	
25	Th		25	Su		25	Tu		25	Fr	
26	Fr		26	Mo	26	26	We		26	Sa	
27	Sa		27	Tu		27	Th		27	Su	
28	Su		28	We		28	Fr		28	Mo	35
29	Mo	22	29	Th		29	Sa		29	Tu	
30	Tu		30	Fr		30	Su		30	We	
31	We					31	Mo	31	31	Th	

Year Planner | Jahresplaner | Planning | Planning **2000**

September			October			November			December		
1	Fr		1	Su		1	We		1	Fr	
2	Sa		2	Mo	40	2	Th		2	Sa	
3	Su		3	Tu		3	Fr		3	Su	
4	Mo	36	4	We		4	Sa		4	Mo	49
5	Tu		5	Th		5	Su		5	Tu	
6	We		6	Fr		6	Mo	45	6	We	
7	Th		7	Sa		7	Tu		7	Th	
8	Fr		8	Su		8	We		8	Fr	
9	Sa		9	Mo	41	9	Th		9	Sa	
10	Su		10	Tu		10	Fr		10	Su	
11	Mo	37	11	We		11	Sa		11	Mo	50
12	Tu		12	Th		12	Su		12	Tu	
13	We		13	Fr		13	Mo	46	13	We	
14	Th		14	Sa		14	Tu		14	Th	
15	Fr		15	Su		15	We		15	Fr	
16	Sa		16	Mo	42	16	Th		16	Sa	
17	Su		17	Tu		17	Fr		17	Su	
18	Mo	38	18	We		18	Sa		18	Mo	51
19	Tu		19	Th		19	Su		19	Tu	
20	We		20	Fr		20	Mo	47	20	We	
21	Th		21	Sa		21	Tu		21	Th	
22	Fr		22	Su		22	We		22	Fr	
23	Sa		23	Mo	43	23	Th		23	Sa	
24	Su		24	Tu		24	Fr		24	Su	
25	Mo	39	25	We		25	Sa		25	Mo	52
26	Tu		26	Th		26	Su		26	Tu	
27	We		27	Fr		27	Mo	48	27	We	
28	Th		28	Sa		28	Tu		28	Th	
29	Fr		29	Su		29	We		29	Fr	
30	Sa		30	Mo	44	30	Th		30	Sa	
			31	Tu					31	Su	

Klimt in the Garden of his Studio | Klimt im Garten seines Ateliers
Klimt dans le jardin de son atelier | Klimt en el jardín de su estudio
Photo: Vienna, Graphische Sammlung Albertina

Music I | Die Musik I
La Musique I | La música I
1895. Oil on canvas, 37 x 44.5 cm
Munich, Bayerische Staatsgemäldesammlungen
Photo: Artothek, Peissenberg / Joachim Blauel

December | Dezember | Décembre | December **1999**

Monday
Montag
Lundi
Maandag

27

Tuesday
Dienstag
Mardi
Dinsdag

28

Wednesday
Mittwoch
Mercredi
Woensdag

29

Thursday
Donnerstag
Jeudi
Donderdag

30

Friday
Freitag
Vendredi
Vrijdag

31

January | Januar | Janvier | Januari **2000**

Saturday
Samstag
Samedi
Zaterdag

1

New Year's Day | Jour de l'An | Neujahr |
Nieuwjaarsdag | Nouvel An | Capo d'Anno

Welcome to the new millenium –
may all your dreams come true!
(and please, continue buying
TASCHEN books. Thank you!)

Week	1	2	3	4	5
Mo·Mo·Lu·Ma	3	10	17	24	31
Tu·Di·Ma·Di	4	11	18	25	1
We·Mi·Me·Wo	5	12	19	26	2
Th·Do·Je·Do	6	13	20	27	3
Fr·Fr·Ve·Vr	7	14	21	28	4
Sa·Sa·Sa·Za	8	15	22	29	5
Su·So·Di·Zo	9	16	23	30	6

2

Sunday
Sonntag
Dimanche
Zondag

January | Januar | Janvier | Januari **2000**

Monday
Montag
Lundi
Maandag

3 0374- 179884.

(UK) (IRL) (NZ) Public Holiday

Tuesday
Dienstag
Mardi
Dinsdag

4

(NZ) Public Holiday

Wednesday
Mittwoch
Mercredi
Woensdag

5

Thursday
Donnerstag
Jeudi
Donderdag

6

(D) Heilige Drei Könige (teilweise)
(A) Heilige Drei Könige

Friday
Freitag
Vendredi
Vrijdag

7

Saturday
Samstag
Samedi
Zaterdag

8

Week		2	3	4	5	6
Mo·Mo·Lu·Ma		10	17	24	31	7
Tu·Di·Ma·Di		11	18	25	1	8
We·Mi·Me·Wo		12	19	26	2	9
Th·Do·Je·Do		13	20	27	3	10
Fr·Fr·Ve·Vr		14	21	28	4	11
Sa·Sa·Sa·Za		15	22	29	5	12
Su·So·Di·Zo		16	23	30	6	13

9 Sunday
Sonntag
Dimanche
Zondag

Finished Drawing for the Allegory "Tragedy" | Reinzeichnung für die Allegorie „Tragödie"
Dessin pour l'allégorie « La tragédie » | Dibujo para la alegoría «Tragedia»
1897. Black crayon and pencil with white chalk and gold, 41.9 x 30.8 cm
Vienna, Historisches Museum der Stadt Wien / Photo: Archiv für Kunst und Geschichte, Berlin

Beethoven Frieze, Hostile Forces (detail) | Beethovenfries, Die feindlichen Gewalten (Detail)
La frise Beethoven, Les Puissances ennemies (détail) | Friso Beethoven, Las fuerzas enemigas (detalle)
1902. Casein colours on stucco with semi-precious inlay and reed base, 220 x 2400 cm
Vienna, Österreichische Galerie im Belvedere / Photo: Artothek, Peissenberg

January | Januar | Janvier | Januari **2000**

Monday
Montag
Lundi
Maandag

10

(i) Coming-of-Age Day

Tuesday
Dienstag
Mardi
Dinsdag

11

Wednesday
Mittwoch
Mercredi
Woensdag

12

Thursday
Donnerstag
Jeudi
Donderdag

13

Friday
Freitag
Vendredi
Vrijdag

14

Saturday
Samstag
Samedi
Zaterdag

15

Week	3	4	5	6	7
Mo·Mo·Lu·Ma	17	24	31	7	14
Tu·Di·Ma·Di	18	25	1	8	15
We·Mi·Me·Wo	19	26	2	9	16
Th·Do·Je·Do	20	27	3	10	17
Fr·Fr·Ve·Vr	21	28	4	11	18
Sa·Sa·Sa·Za	22	29	5	12	19
Su·So·Di·Zo	23	30	6	13	20

16

Sunday
Sonntag
Dimanche
Zondag

January | Januar | Janvier | Januari **2000**

Monday
Montag
Lundi
Maandag

17

(USA) Martin Luther King Day

Tuesday
Dienstag
Mardi
Dinsdag

18

Wednesday
Mittwoch
Mercredi
Woensdag

19

Thursday
Donnerstag
Jeudi
Donderdag

20

Friday
Freitag
Vendredi
Vrijdag

21

Saturday
Samstag
Samedi
Zaterdag

22

(IL) Tu B'Shevat

Week		4	5	6	7	8
Mo·Mo·Lu·Ma		24	31	7	14	21
Tu·Di·Ma·Di		25	1	8	15	22
We·Mi·Me·Wo		26	2	9	16	23
Th·Do·Je·Do		27	3	10	17	24
Fr·Fr·Ve·Vr		28	4	11	18	25
Sa·Sa·Sa·Za		29	5	12	19	26
Su·So·Di·Zo		30	6	13	20	27

23

Sunday
Sonntag
Dimanche
Zondag

Portrait of a Lady (Frau Heymann?) | Damenbildnis (Frau Heymann?)
Portrait de femme (portrait de Madame Heymann?) | Retrato femenino (¿retrato de la Sra. Heymann?)
c. 1894. Oil on wood, 39 x 23 cm
Vienna, Historisches Museum der Stadt Wien / Photo: Archiv für Kunst und Geschichte, Berlin

Music | Die Musik
La Musique | La música
1901. Lithograph
Vienna, Graphische Sammlung Albertina

January | Januar | Janvier | Januari **2000**

Monday
Montag
Lundi
Maandag

24

Tuesday
Dienstag
Mardi
Dinsdag

25

Wednesday
Mittwoch
Mercredi
Woensdag

26

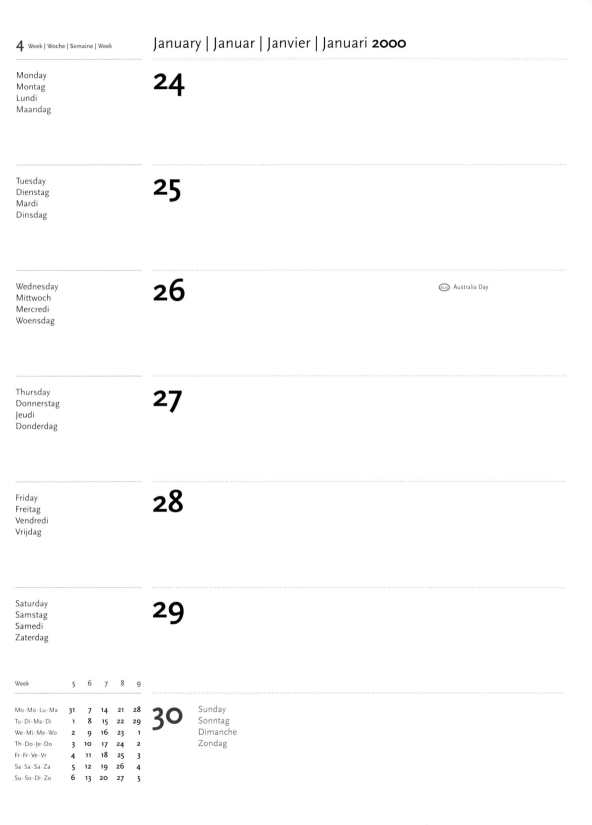 AUS Australia Day

Thursday
Donnerstag
Jeudi
Donderdag

27

Friday
Freitag
Vendredi
Vrijdag

28

Saturday
Samstag
Samedi
Zaterdag

29

Week	5	6	7	8	9
Mo·Mo·Lu·Ma	31	7	14	21	28
Tu·Di·Ma·Di	1	8	15	22	29
We·Mi·Me·Wo	2	9	16	23	1
Th·Do·Je·Do	3	10	17	24	2
Fr·Fr·Ve·Vr	4	11	18	25	3
Sa·Sa·Sa·Za	5	12	19	26	4
Su·So·Di·Zo	6	13	20	27	5

30 Sunday
Sonntag
Dimanche
Zondag

January | Januar | Janvier | Januari **2000**

Monday
Montag
Lundi
Maandag

31

February | Februar | Février | Februari **2000**

Tuesday
Dienstag
Mardi
Dinsdag

1

Wednesday
Mittwoch
Mercredi
Woensdag

2

Thursday
Donnerstag
Jeudi
Donderdag

3

Friday
Freitag
Vendredi
Vrijdag

4

Saturday
Samstag
Samedi
Zaterdag

5

Week	6	7	8	9	10
Mo · Mo · Lu · Ma	7	14	21	28	6
Tu · Di · Ma · Di	8	15	22	29	7
We · Mi · Me · Wo	9	16	23	1	8
Th · Do · Je · Do	10	17	24	2	9
Fr · Fr · Ve · Vr	11	18	25	3	10
Sa · Sa · Sa · Za	12	19	26	4	11
Su · So · Di · Zo	13	20	27	5	12

6

Sunday
Sonntag
Dimanche
Zondag

(NZ) Waitangi Day

Woman Seated with Thighs apart | Sitzende Frau mit gespreizten Schenkeln
Femme assise aux cuisses écartées | Mujer sentada con los muslos separados
1916/17. Pencil, red coloured pencil, white highlights, 57 x 37.5 cm
Private collection

Nuda Veritas (detail)
1899. Oil on canvas, 252 x 56 cm
Vienna, Österreichische Galerie im Belvedere / Photo: Archiv für Kunst und Geschichte, Berlin

February | Februar | Février | Februari **2000**

Monday
Montag
Lundi
Maandag

7

Tuesday
Dienstag
Mardi
Dinsdag

8

Wednesday
Mittwoch
Mercredi
Woensdag

9

Thursday
Donnerstag
Jeudi
Donderdag

10

Publisher's birthday.
Please send your congratulations to:
Benedikt Taschen,
fax number: +49 221 254919,
email: b.taschen@taschen.com,
Hohenzollernring 53, D–50672 Cologne

Friday
Freitag
Vendredi
Vrijdag

11

(i) Commemoration of the
Founding of the Nation

Saturday
Samstag
Samedi
Zaterdag

12

Week	7	8	9	10	11
Mo·Mo·Lu·Ma	14	21	28	6	13
Tu·Di·Ma·Di	15	22	29	7	14
We·Mi·Me·Wo	16	23	1	8	15
Th·Do·Je·Do	17	24	2	9	16
Fr·Fr·Ve·Vr	18	25	3	10	17
Sa·Sa·Sa·Za	19	26	4	11	18
Su·So·Di·Zo	20	27	5	12	19

13 Sunday
Sonntag
Dimanche
Zondag

February | Februar | Février | Februari **2000**

Monday
Montag
Lundi
Maandag

14

Tuesday
Dienstag
Mardi
Dinsdag

15

Wednesday
Mittwoch
Mercredi
Woensdag

16

Thursday
Donnerstag
Jeudi
Donderdag

17

Friday
Freitag
Vendredi
Vrijdag

18

Saturday
Samstag
Samedi
Zaterdag

19

Week	8	9	10	11	12
Mo·Mo·Lu·Ma	21	28	6	13	20
Tu·Di·Ma·Di	22	29	7	14	21
We·Mi·Me·Wo	23	1	8	15	22
Th·Do·Je·Do	24	2	9	16	23
Fr·Fr·Ve·Vr	25	3	10	17	24
Sa·Sa·Sa·Za	26	4	11	18	25
Su·So·Di·Zo	27	5	12	19	26

20
Sunday
Sonntag
Dimanche
Zondag

Beethoven Frieze, Ode to Joy (detail) | Beethovenfries, Freude, schöner Götterfunken (Detail)
La frise Beethoven, Joie, belle étincelle divine (détail) | Friso Beethoven, Alegría, inspiración divina (detalle)
1902. Casein colours on stucco with semi-precious inlay and reed base, 220 x 2400 cm
Vienna, Österreichische Galerie im Belvedere / Photo: Archiv für Kunst und Geschichte, Berlin / Erich Lessing

Judith I
1901. Oil on canvas, 84 x 42 cm
Vienna, Österreichische Galerie im Belvedere

February | Februar | Février | Februari **2000**

Monday
Montag
Lundi
Maandag

21   ⬭USA Presidents' Day

Tuesday
Dienstag
Mardi
Dinsdag

22

Wednesday
Mittwoch
Mercredi
Woensdag

23

Thursday
Donnerstag
Jeudi
Donderdag

24

Friday
Freitag
Vendredi
Vrijdag

25

Saturday
Samstag
Samedi
Zaterdag

26

Week	9	10	11	12	13
Mo·Mo·Lu·Ma	28	6	13	20	27
Tu·Di·Ma·Di	29	7	14	21	28
We·Mi·Me·Wo	1	8	15	22	29
Th·Do·Je·Do	2	9	16	23	30
Fr·Fr·Ve·Vr	3	10	17	24	31
Sa·Sa·Sa·Za	4	11	18	25	1
Su·So·Di·Zo	5	12	19	26	2

27 Sunday
Sonntag
Dimanche
Zondag

February | Februar | Février | Februari 2000

Monday
Montag
Lundi
Maandag

28

Tuesday
Dienstag
Mardi
Dinsdag

29

March | März | Mars | Maart 2000

Wednesday
Mittwoch
Mercredi
Woensdag

1

Thursday
Donnerstag
Jeudi
Donderdag

2

Friday
Freitag
Vendredi
Vrijdag

3

Saturday
Samstag
Samedi
Zaterdag

4

Week	10	11	12	13	14
Mo·Mo·Lu·Ma	6	13	20	27	3
Tu·Di·Ma·Di	7	14	21	28	4
We·Mi·Me·Wo	8	15	22	29	5
Th·Do·Je·Do	9	16	23	30	6
Fr·Fr·Ve·Vr	10	17	24	31	7
Sa·Sa·Sa·Za	11	18	25	1	8
Su·So·Di·Zo	12	19	26	2	9

5

Sunday
Sonntag
Dimanche
Zondag

Emilie Flöge
1909. Photo: Dora Bender
Österreichische NationalBibliothek / © Photo: Bildarchiv / ÖNB, Wien

Portrait of Emilie Flöge | Bildnis Emilie Flöge
Portrait d'Emilie Flöge | Retrato de Emilie Flöge
1902. Oil on canvas, 181 x 84 cm
Vienna, Historisches Museum der Stadt Wien

March | März | Mars | Maart **2000**

Monday Montag Lundi Maandag	**6**

Tuesday Dienstag Mardi Dinsdag	**7**

Wednesday Mittwoch Mercredi Woensdag	**8**

Thursday Donnerstag Jeudi Donderdag	**9**

Friday Freitag Vendredi Vrijdag	**10**

Saturday Samstag Samedi Zaterdag	**11**

Week	11	12	13	14	15
Mo·Mo·Lu·Ma	13	20	27	3	10
Tu·Di·Ma·Di	14	21	28	4	11
We·Mi·Me·Wo	15	22	29	5	12
Th·Do·Je·Do	16	23	30	6	13
Fr·Fr·Ve·Vr	17	24	31	7	14
Sa·Sa·Sa·Za	18	25	1	8	15
Su·So·Di·Zo	19	26	2	9	16

12	Sunday Sonntag Dimanche Zondag

March | März | Mars | Maart **2000**

Monday
Montag
Lundi
Maandag

13

Tuesday
Dienstag
Mardi
Dinsdag

14

Wednesday
Mittwoch
Mercredi
Woensdag

15

Thursday
Donnerstag
Jeudi
Donderdag

16

Friday
Freitag
Vendredi
Vrijdag

17

(UK) Saint Patrick's Day
(Northern Ireland only)
(IRL) Saint Patrick's Day

Saturday
Samstag
Samedi
Zaterdag

18

Week		12	13	14	15	16
Mo·Mo·Lu·Ma		20	27	3	10	17
Tu·Di·Ma·Di		21	28	4	11	18
We·Mi·Me·Wo		22	29	5	12	19
Th·Do·Je·Do		23	30	6	13	20
Fr·Fr·Ve·Vr		24	31	7	14	21
Sa·Sa·Sa·Za		25	1	8	15	22
Su·So·Di·Zo		26	2	9	16	23

19 Sunday
Sonntag
Dimanche
Zondag

Love | Liebe | L'Amour | Amor
1895. Oil on canvas, 60 x 44 cm
Vienna, Historisches Museum der Stadt Wien
Photo: Archiv für Kunst und Geschichte, Berlin/Erich Lessing

Beethoven Frieze, Ode to Joy (detail) | Beethovenfries, Freude, schöner Götterfunken (Detail)
La frise Beethoven, Joie, belle étincelle divine (détail) | Friso Beethoven, Alegría, inspiración divina (detalle)
1902. Casein colours on stucco with semi-precious inlay and reed base, 220 x 2400 cm
Vienna, Österreichische Galerie im Belvedere

March | März | Mars | Maart **2000**

Monday
Montag
Lundi
Maandag

20

ⓘ Vernal Equinox Day

Tuesday
Dienstag
Mardi
Dinsdag

21

ⓩⓐ Human Rights Day
ⓘⓛ Purim

Wednesday
Mittwoch
Mercredi
Woensdag

22

Thursday
Donnerstag
Jeudi
Donderdag

23

Friday
Freitag
Vendredi
Vrijdag

24

Saturday
Samstag
Samedi
Zaterdag

25

Week	13	14	15	16	17
Mo · Mo · Lu · Ma	27	3	10	17	24
Tu · Di · Ma · Di	28	4	11	18	25
We · Mi · Me · Wo	29	5	12	19	26
Th · Do · Je · Do	30	6	13	20	27
Fr · Fr · Ve · Vr	31	7	14	21	28
Sa · Sa · Sa · Za	1	8	15	22	29
Su · So · Di · Zo	2	9	16	23	30

26

Sunday
Sonntag
Dimanche
Zondag

March | März | Mars | Maart **2000**

Monday
Montag
Lundi
Maandag

27

Tuesday
Dienstag
Mardi
Dinsdag

28

Wednesday
Mittwoch
Mercredi
Woensdag

29

Thursday
Donnerstag
Jeudi
Donderdag

30

Friday
Freitag
Vendredi
Vrijdag

31

April | April | Avril | April **2000**

Saturday
Samstag
Samedi
Zaterdag

1

Week	14	15	16	17	18
Mo·Mo·Lu·Ma	3	10	17	24	1
Tu·Di·Ma·Di	4	11	18	25	2
We·Mi·Me·Wo	5	12	19	26	3
Th·Do·Je·Do	6	13	20	27	4
Fr·Fr·Ve·Vr	7	14	21	28	5
Sa·Sa·Sa·Za	8	15	22	29	6
Su·So·Di·Zo	9	16	23	30	7

2 Sunday
Sonntag
Dimanche
Zondag

After the Rain (Garden with Chickens in St Agatha) | Nach dem Regen (Garten mit Hühnern in St. Agatha)
Après la pluie (Jardin aux poules à St Agatha) | Después de la lluvia (Huerta con gallinas en Sta. Ágata)
1899. Oil on canvas, 80 x 40 cm
Vienna, Österreichische Galerie im Belvedere / Photo: Archiv für Kunst und Geschichte, Berlin

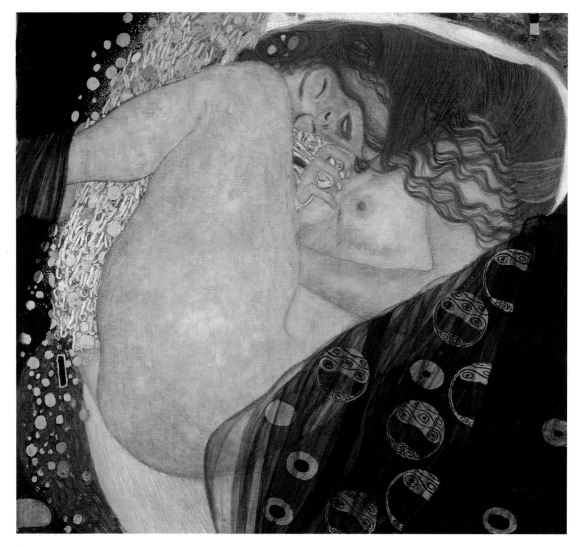

Danae
c. 1907/08. Oil on canvas, 77 x 83 cm
Private collection / Photo: Artothek, Peissenberg / Brandstätter

April | April | Avril | April **2000**

Monday
Montag
Lundi
Maandag

3

Tuesday
Dienstag
Mardi
Dinsdag

4

Wednesday
Mittwoch
Mercredi
Woensdag

5

Thursday
Donnerstag
Jeudi
Donderdag

6

Friday
Freitag
Vendredi
Vrijdag

7

Saturday
Samstag
Samedi
Zaterdag

8

Week	15	16	17	18	19
Mo·Mo·Lu·Ma	10	17	24	1	8
Tu·Di·Ma·Di	11	18	25	2	9
We·Mi·Me·Wo	12	19	26	3	10
Th·Do·Je·Do	13	20	27	4	11
Fr·Fr·Ve·Vr	14	21	28	5	12
Sa·Sa·Sa·Za	15	22	29	6	13
Su·So·Di·Zo	16	23	30	7	14

9

Sunday
Sonntag
Dimanche
Zondag

April | April | Avril | April **2000**

Monday
Montag
Lundi
Maandag

10

Tuesday
Dienstag
Mardi
Dinsdag

11

Wednesday
Mittwoch
Mercredi
Woensdag

12

Thursday
Donnerstag
Jeudi
Donderdag

13

Friday
Freitag
Vendredi
Vrijdag

14

Saturday
Samstag
Samedi
Zaterdag

15

Week	16	17	18	19	20
Mo·Mo·Lu·Ma	17	24	1	8	15
Tu·Di·Ma·Di	18	25	2	9	16
We·Mi·Me·Wo	19	26	3	10	17
Th·Do·Je·Do	20	27	4	11	18
Fr·Fr·Ve·Vr	21	28	5	12	19
Sa·Sa·Sa·Za	22	29	6	13	20
Su·So·Di·Zo	23	30	7	14	21

16 Sunday
Sonntag
Dimanche
Zondag

The Three Ages of Woman | Die drei Lebensalter der Frau
Les Trois Ages de la femme | Las tres edades de la vida
1905. Oil on canvas, 180 x 180 cm
Rome, Galleria Nazionale d'Arte Moderna / Photo: Artothek, Peissenberg

Expectation (Working Design for Stoclet Frieze) | Die Erwartung (Werkvorlage zum Stoclet-Fries)
L'Attente (projet d'œuvre pour la frise Stoclet) | La expectación (modelo para el Friso Stoclet)
c. 1905–1909. Tempera, watercolour, gold paint, silver-bronze, crayon, pencil, opaque white, gold leaf and silver leaf on paper, 193 x 115 cm
Vienna, Österreichisches Museum für Angewandte Kunst / Photo: Artothek, Peissenberg

April | April | Avril | April **2000**

Monday
Montag
Lundi
Maandag

17

Tuesday
Dienstag
Mardi
Dinsdag

18

Wednesday
Mittwoch
Mercredi
Woensdag

19

Thursday
Donnerstag
Jeudi
Donderdag

20

(IL) Passover

Friday
Freitag
Vendredi
Vrijdag

21

(UK) (CAN) (NZ) (AUS) (ZA) (D) (CH) (NL)
Good Friday | Vendredi Saint | Karfreitag |
Goede Vrijdag | Venerdi Santo

Saturday
Samstag
Samedi
Zaterdag

22

Week	17	18	19	20	21
Mo·Mo·Lu·Ma	24	1	8	15	22
Tu·Di·Ma·Di	25	2	9	16	23
We·Mi·Me·Wo	26	3	10	17	24
Th·Do·Je·Do	27	4	11	18	25
Fr·Fr·Ve·Vr	28	5	12	19	26
Sa·Sa·Sa·Za	29	6	13	20	27
Su·So·Di·Zo	30	7	14	21	28

23 Sunday
Sonntag
Dimanche
Zondag

Easter Sunday | Pâques | Ostersonntag |
1° Paasdag | Pasen | Pasqua

April | April | Avril | April **2000**

Monday
Montag
Lundi
Maandag

24

(UK) Easter Monday (except Scotland)
(IRL) (NZ) (AUS) (ZA) (F) (D) (A)
(CH) (NL) (B)
Easter Monday | Family Day | Lundi de
Pâques | Ostermontag | 2ᵉ Paasdag |
Paasmaandag | Lunedì dell'Angelo

Tuesday
Dienstag
Mardi
Dinsdag

25

(NZ) (AUS) Anzac Day

Wednesday
Mittwoch
Mercredi
Woensdag

26

Thursday
Donnerstag
Jeudi
Donderdag

27

(ZA) Constitution Day

Friday
Freitag
Vendredi
Vrijdag

28

Saturday
Samstag
Samedi
Zaterdag

29

(J) Greenery Day

Week	18	19	20	21	22
Mo·Mo·Lu·Ma	1	8	15	22	29
Tu·Di·Ma·Di	2	9	16	23	30
We·Mi·Me·Wo	3	10	17	24	31
Th·Do·Je·Do	4	11	18	25	1
Fr·Fr·Ve·Vr	5	12	19	26	2
Sa·Sa·Sa·Za	6	13	20	27	3
Su·So·Di·Zo	7	14	21	28	4

30

Sunday
Sonntag
Dimanche
Zondag

(NL) Koninginnedag

Klimt in the Garden of his Studio | Klimt im Garten seines Ateliers
Klimt dans le jardin de son atelier | Klimt en el jardín de su estudio

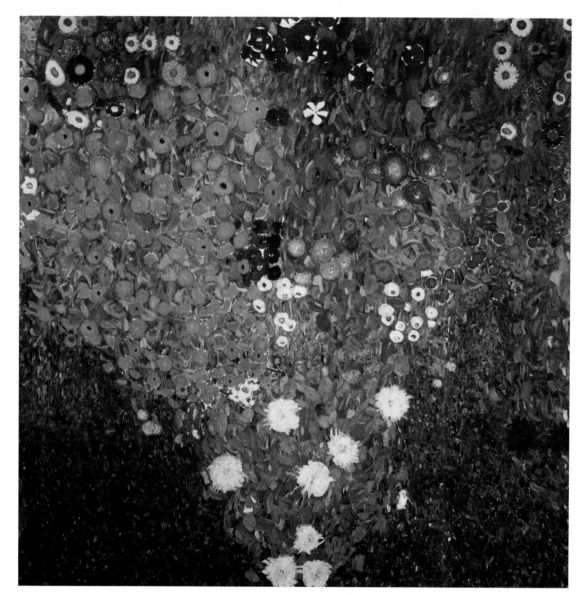

Farm Garden (Flower Garden) | Bauerngarten (Blumengarten)
Le Jardin fleuri | Jardín
1905/06. Oil on canvas, 110 x 110 cm
Prague, Národni Galerie

Monday
Montag
Lundi
Maandag

1

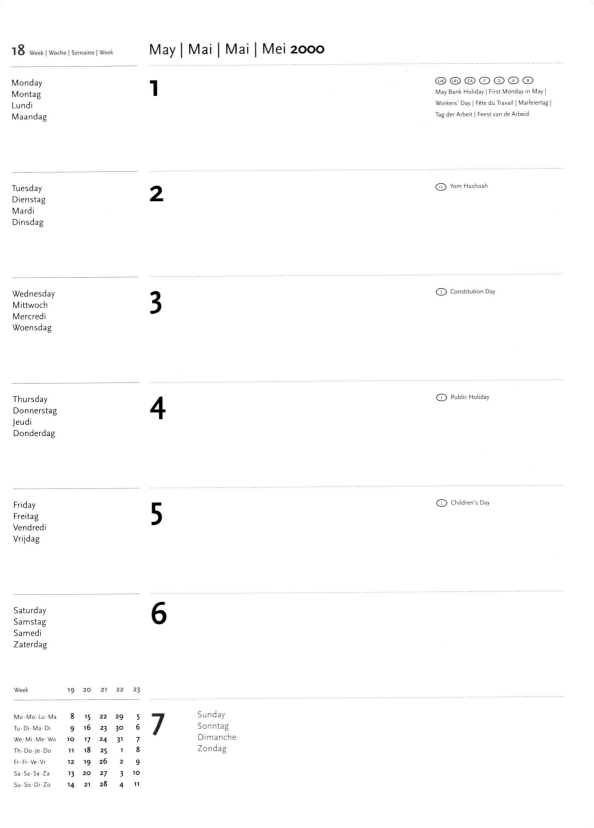

(UK) (IRL) (ZA) (F) (D) (A) (B)
May Bank Holiday | First Monday in May |
Workers' Day | Fête du Travail | Maifeiertag |
Tag der Arbeit | Feest van de Arbeid

Tuesday
Dienstag
Mardi
Dinsdag

2

(IL) Yom Hashoah

Wednesday
Mittwoch
Mercredi
Woensdag

3

(J) Constitution Day

Thursday
Donnerstag
Jeudi
Donderdag

4

(J) Public Holiday

Friday
Freitag
Vendredi
Vrijdag

5

(J) Children's Day

Saturday
Samstag
Samedi
Zaterdag

6

Week	19	20	21	22	23
Mo · Mo · Lu · Ma	8	15	22	29	5
Tu · Di · Ma · Di	9	16	23	30	6
We · Mi · Me · Wo	10	17	24	31	7
Th · Do · Je · Do	11	18	25	1	8
Fr · Fr · Ve · Vr	12	19	26	2	9
Sa · Sa · Sa · Za	13	20	27	3	10
Su · So · Di · Zo	14	21	28	4	11

7

Sunday
Sonntag
Dimanche
Zondag

May | Mai | Mai | Mei **2000**

Monday
Montag
Lundi
Maandag

8

F Fête de la Libération

Tuesday
Dienstag
Mardi
Dinsdag

9

Wednesday
Mittwoch
Mercredi
Woensdag

10

IL Yom Haatzmaut

Thursday
Donnerstag
Jeudi
Donderdag

11

Friday
Freitag
Vendredi
Vrijdag

12

Saturday
Samstag
Samedi
Zaterdag

13

Week	20	21	22	23	24
Mo·Mo·Lu·Ma	15	22	29	5	12
Tu·Di·Ma·Di	16	23	30	6	13
We·Mi·Me·Wo	17	24	31	7	14
Th·Do·Je·Do	18	25	1	8	15
Fr·Fr·Ve·Vr	19	26	2	9	16
Sa·Sa·Sa·Za	20	27	3	10	17
Su·So·Di·Zo	21	28	4	11	18

14 Sunday
Sonntag
Dimanche
Zondag

Poppy Field | Mohnwiese
Le Champ de coquelicots | Prado con amapolas
1907. Oil on canvas, 110 x 110 cm
Vienna, Österreichische Galerie im Belvedere
Photo: Archiv für Kunst und Geschichte, Berlin / Erich Lessing

Portrait of Fritza Riedler | Bildnis Fritza Riedler
Portrait de Fritza Riedler | Retrato de Fritza Riedler
1906. Oil on canvas, 153 x 133 cm
Vienna, Österreichische Galerie im Belvedere

May | Mai | Mai | Mei **2000**

Monday
Montag
Lundi
Maandag

15

Tuesday
Dienstag
Mardi
Dinsdag

16

Wednesday
Mittwoch
Mercredi
Woensdag

17

Thursday
Donnerstag
Jeudi
Donderdag

18

Friday
Freitag
Vendredi
Vrijdag

19

Saturday
Samstag
Samedi
Zaterdag

20

Week	21	22	23	24	25
Mo·Mo·Lu·Ma	22	29	5	12	19
Tu·Di·Ma·Di	23	30	6	13	20
We·Mi·Me·Wo	24	31	7	14	21
Th·Do·Je·Do	25	1	8	15	22
Fr·Fr·Ve·Vr	26	2	9	16	23
Sa·Sa·Sa·Za	27	3	10	17	24
Su·So·Di·Zo	28	4	11	18	25

21

Sunday
Sonntag
Dimanche
Zondag

May | Mai | Mai | Mei **2000**

Monday Montag Lundi Maandag	**22**	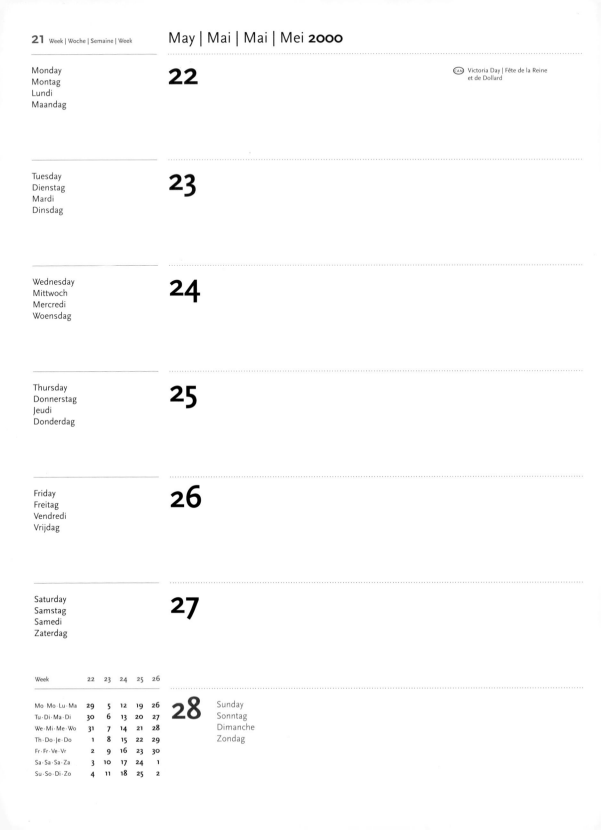 (CAN) Victoria Day	Fête de la Reine et de Dollard

Tuesday
Dienstag
Mardi
Dinsdag

23

Wednesday
Mittwoch
Mercredi
Woensdag

24

Thursday
Donnerstag
Jeudi
Donderdag

25

Friday
Freitag
Vendredi
Vrijdag

26

Saturday
Samstag
Samedi
Zaterdag

27

Week	22	23	24	25	26
Mo Mo·Lu·Ma	29	5	12	19	26
Tu·Di·Ma·Di	30	6	13	20	27
We·Mi·Me·Wo	31	7	14	21	28
Th·Do·Je·Do	1	8	15	22	29
Fr·Fr·Ve·Vr	2	9	16	23	30
Sa·Sa·Sa·Za	3	10	17	24	1
Su·So·Di·Zo	4	11	18	25	2

28 Sunday
Sonntag
Dimanche
Zondag

Poster for the "Ist Secession" exhibition (before censorship) | Plakat für die Ausstellung der „I. Secession" (vor der Zensur)
Affiche d'exposition pour la « Sécession I » (avant la censure) | Cartel para la Exposición de la «Iª Secession» (antes de pasar por la censura)
1898. Lithograph, 62 x 43 cm
New York, Private collection, by permission of Barry Friedman Ltd.

Beethoven Frieze, Hostile Forces (detail) | Beethovenfries, Die feindlichen Gewalten (Detail)
La frise Beethoven, Les Puissances ennemies (détail) | Friso Beethoven, Las fuerzas enemigas (detalle)
1902. Casein colours on stucco with semi-precious inlay and reed base, 220 x 2400 cm
Vienna, Österreichische Galerie im Belvedere

May | Mai | Mai | Mei **2000**

Monday Montag Lundi Maandag	**29**	ⓤ Memorial Day ⓤ Spring Bank Holiday
Tuesday Dienstag Mardi Dinsdag	**30**	
Wednesday Mittwoch Mercredi Woensdag	**31**	

June | Juni | Juin | Juni **2000**

Thursday Donnerstag Jeudi Donderdag	**1**	Ⓕ Ⓓ Ⓐ ⒸⒽ ⓃⓁ Ⓑ Ascension | Christi Himmelfahrt | Auffahrt | Hemelvaartsdag | Onze-Lieve-Heer-Hemelvaart | Ascensione
Friday Freitag Vendredi Vrijdag	**2**	
Saturday Samstag Samedi Zaterdag	**3**	

Week	23	24	25	26	27
Mo·Mo·Lu·Ma	5	12	19	26	3
Tu·Di·Ma·Di	6	13	20	27	4
We·Mi·Me·Wo	7	14	21	28	5
Th·Do·Je·Do	8	15	22	29	6
Fr·Fr·Ve·Vr	9	16	23	30	7
Sa·Sa·Sa·Za	10	17	24	1	8
Su·So·Di·Zo	11	18	25	2	9

4 Sunday
Sonntag
Dimanche
Zondag

June | Juni | Juin | Juni **2000**

Monday
Montag
Lundi
Maandag

5

IRL First Monday in June
NZ Queen's Birthday

Tuesday
Dienstag
Mardi
Dinsdag

6

Wednesday
Mittwoch
Mercredi
Woensdag

7

Thursday
Donnerstag
Jeudi
Donderdag

8

Friday
Freitag
Vendredi
Vrijdag

9

IL Shavuot

Saturday
Samstag
Samedi
Zaterdag

10

Week	24	25	26	27	28
Mo · Mo · Lu · Ma	12	19	26	3	10
Tu · Di · Ma · Di	13	20	27	4	11
We · Mi · Me · Wo	14	21	28	5	12
Th · Do · Je · Do	15	22	29	6	13
Fr · Fr · Ve · Vr	16	23	30	7	14
Sa · Sa · Sa · Za	17	24	1	8	15
Su · So · Di · Zo	18	25	2	9	16

11 Sunday
Sonntag
Dimanche
Zondag

Pentecôte | Pfingstsonntag | 1e Pinksterdag |
Pinksteren | Pentecoste

Portrait of Sonja Knips | Bildnis Sonja Knips
Portrait de Sonja Knips | Retrato de Sonja Knips
1898. Oil on canvas, 145 x 146 cm
Vienna, Österreichische Galerie im Belvedere
Photo: Archiv für Kunst und Geschichte, Berlin / Erich Lessing

Portrait of Mäda Primavesi | Bildnis Mäda Primavesi
Portrait de Mäda Primavesi | Retrato de Mäda Primavesi
1912. Oil on canvas, 150 x 110.5 cm
New York, The Metropolitan Museum of Art

June | Juni | Juin | Juni **2000**

Monday Montag Lundi Maandag	**12**

F D A CH NL B
Lundi de Pentecôte | Pfingstmontag |
2e Pinksterdag | Pinkstermaandag |
Lunedì di Pentecoste

Tuesday
Dienstag
Mardi
Dinsdag — **13**

Wednesday
Mittwoch
Mercredi
Woensdag — **14**

Thursday
Donnerstag
Jeudi
Donderdag — **15**

Friday
Freitag
Vendredi
Vrijdag — **16** ZA Youth Day

Saturday
Samstag
Samedi
Zaterdag — **17**

Week	25	26	27	28	29
Mo·Mo·Lu·Ma	19	26	3	10	17
Tu·Di·Ma·Di	20	27	4	11	18
We·Mi·Me·Wo	21	28	5	12	19
Th·Do·Je·Do	22	29	6	13	20
Fr·Fr·Ve·Vr	23	30	7	14	21
Sa·Sa·Sa·Za	24	1	8	15	22
Su·So·Di·Zo	25	2	9	16	23

18 Sunday
Sonntag
Dimanche
Zondag

June | Juni | Juin | Juni **2000**

Monday
Montag
Lundi
Maandag

19

Tuesday
Dienstag
Mardi
Dinsdag

20

Wednesday
Mittwoch
Mercredi
Woensdag

21

Thursday
Donnerstag
Jeudi
Donderdag

22

Ⓓ Fronleichnam (teilweise)
Ⓐ Fronleichnam

Friday
Freitag
Vendredi
Vrijdag

23

Saturday
Samstag
Samedi
Zaterdag

24

ⒸAN Québec's National Holiday |
Fête Nationale du Québec

Week	26	27	28	29	30
Mo·Mo·Lu·Ma	26	3	10	17	24
Tu·Di·Ma·Di	27	4	11	18	25
We·Mi·Me·Wo	28	5	12	19	26
Th·Do·Je·Do	29	6	13	20	27
Fr·Fr·Ve·Vr	30	7	14	21	28
Sa·Sa·Sa·Za	1	8	15	22	29
Su·So·Di·Zo	2	9	16	23	30

25

Sunday
Sonntag
Dimanche
Zondag

Avenue in the Park of Schloss Kammer | Allee im Park von Schloß Kammer
Allée du parc du château Kammer | Paseo en el parque del palacio Kammer
1912. Oil on canvas, 110 x 110 cm
Vienna, Österreichische Galerie im Belvedere
Photo: Archiv für Kunst und Geschichte, Berlin

The Girlfriends | Die Freundinnen
Les Amies | Las amigas
1916/17. Oil on canvas, 99 x 99 cm
Vienna, Österreichische Galerie im Belvedere

June | Juni | Juin | Juni **2000**

Monday
Montag
Lundi
Maandag

26

Tuesday
Dienstag
Mardi
Dinsdag

27

Wednesday
Mittwoch
Mercredi
Woensdag

28

Thursday
Donnerstag
Jeudi
Donderdag

29

Friday
Freitag
Vendredi
Vrijdag

30

July | Juli | Juillet | Juli **2000**

Saturday
Samstag
Samedi
Zaterdag

1

CAN Canada Day | Jour de la Confédération

Week		27	28	29	30	31
Mo·Mo·Lu·Ma	3	10	17	24	31
Tu·Di·Ma·Di	4	11	18	25	1
We·Mi·Me·Wo	5	12	19	26	2
Th·Do·Je·Do	6	13	20	27	3
Fr·Fr·Ve·Vr	7	14	21	28	4
Sa·Sa·Sa·Za	8	15	22	29	5
Su·So·Di·Zo	9	16	23	30	6

2

Sunday
Sonntag
Dimanche
Zondag

July | Juli | Juillet | Juli **2000**

Monday
Montag
Lundi
Maandag

3

Tuesday
Dienstag
Mardi
Dinsdag

4

(USA) Independence Day

Wednesday
Mittwoch
Mercredi
Woensdag

5

Thursday
Donnerstag
Jeudi
Donderdag

6

Friday
Freitag
Vendredi
Vrijdag

7

Saturday
Samstag
Samedi
Zaterdag

8

Week	28	29	30	31	32
Mo·Mo·Lu·Ma	10	17	24	31	7
Tu·Di·Ma·Di	11	18	25	1	8
We·Mi·Me·Wo	12	19	26	2	9
Th·Do·Je·Do	13	20	27	3	10
Fr·Fr·Ve·Vr	14	21	28	4	11
Sa·Sa·Sa·Za	15	22	29	5	12
Su·So·Di·Zo	16	23	30	6	13

9

Sunday
Sonntag
Dimanche
Zondag

Schloss Kammer on the Attersee I | Schloß Kammer am Attersee I
Château Kammer sur l'Attersee I | Palacio Kammer a orillas del Lago Atter I
c. 1908. Oil on canvas, 110 x 110 cm
Prague, Národni Galerie / Photo: Artothek, Peissenberg

Fulfilment (Working design for the Stoclet Frieze, detail) | Die Erfüllung (Werkvorlage zum Stoclet-Fries, Detail)
L'Accomplissement (projet d'œuvre pour la frise Stoclet, détail) | La satisfacción (modelo para el Friso Stoclet, detalle)
c. 1905–1909. Tempera, watercolour, gold paint, silver-bronze, crayon, pencil, opaque white, gold leaf and silver leaf on paper, 194 x 121 cm
Vienna, Österreichisches Museum für Angewandte Kunst / Photo: Archiv für Kunst und Geschichte, Berlin

July | Juli | Juillet | Juli **2000**

Monday
Montag
Lundi
Maandag

10

Tuesday
Dienstag
Mardi
Dinsdag

11

Wednesday
Mittwoch
Mercredi
Woensdag

12

Thursday
Donnerstag
Jeudi
Donderdag

13

Friday
Freitag
Vendredi
Vrijdag

14

ⓕ Fête Nationale

Saturday
Samstag
Samedi
Zaterdag

15

Week	29	30	31	32	33
Mo·Mo·Lu·Ma	17	24	31	7	14
Tu·Di·Ma·Di	18	25	1	8	15
We·Mi·Me·Wo	19	26	2	9	16
Th·Do·Je·Do	20	27	3	10	17
Fr·Fr·Ve·Vr	21	28	4	11	18
Sa·Sa·Sa·Za	22	29	5	12	19
Su·So·Di·Zo	23	30	6	13	20

16

Sunday
Sonntag
Dimanche
Zondag

July | Juli | Juillet | Juli **2000**

Monday
Montag
Lundi
Maandag

17

Tuesday
Dienstag
Mardi
Dinsdag

18

Wednesday
Mittwoch
Mercredi
Woensdag

19

Thursday
Donnerstag
Jeudi
Donderdag

20

(J) Marine Day

Friday
Freitag
Vendredi
Vrijdag

21

(B) Nationale Feestdag | Fête Nationale

Saturday
Samstag
Samedi
Zaterdag

22

Week	30	31	32	33	34
Mo·Mo·Lu·Ma	24	31	7	14	21
Tu·Di·Ma·Di	25	1	8	15	22
We·Mi·Me·Wo	26	2	9	16	23
Th·Do·Je·Do	27	3	10	17	24
Fr·Fr·Ve·Vr	28	4	11	18	25
Sa·Sa·Sa·Za	29	5	12	19	26
Su·So·Di·Zo	30	6	13	20	27

23

Sunday
Sonntag
Dimanche
Zondag

Portrait of a Lady | Damenbildnis
Portrait de femme | Retrato femenino
1917/18. Oil on canvas, 180 x 90 cm
Linz, Neue Galerie der Stadt Linz, Wolfgang-Gurlitt-Museum

Black Feather Hat (Lady with Feather Hat) | **Der schwarze Federhut (Dame mit Federhut)**
Le Chapeau de plumes noires | **El sombrero de plumas negro (Dama con sombrero de plumas)**
1910. Oil on canvas, 79 x 63 cm
Private collection / Photo: Artothek, Peissenberg

Monday
Montag
Lundi
Maandag

24

Tuesday
Dienstag
Mardi
Dinsdag

25

Wednesday
Mittwoch
Mercredi
Woensdag

26

Thursday
Donnerstag
Jeudi
Donderdag

27

Friday
Freitag
Vendredi
Vrijdag

28

Saturday
Samstag
Samedi
Zaterdag

29

Week	31	32	33	34	35
Mo·Mo·Lu·Ma	31	7	14	21	28
Tu·Di·Ma·Di	1	8	15	22	29
We·Mi·Me·Wo	2	9	16	23	30
Th·Do·Je·Do	3	10	17	24	31
Fr·Fr·Ve·Vr	4	11	18	25	1
Sa·Sa·Sa·Za	5	12	19	26	2
Su·So·Di·Zo	6	13	20	27	3

30 Sunday
Sonntag
Dimanche
Zondag

July | Juli | Juillet | Juli 2000

Monday
Montag
Lundi
Maandag

31

August | August | Août | Augustus 2000

Tuesday
Dienstag
Mardi
Dinsdag

1

CH Bundesfeiertag | Fête nationale suisse |
Festa nazionale svizzera

Wednesday
Mittwoch
Mercredi
Woensdag

2

Thursday
Donnerstag
Jeudi
Donderdag

3

Friday
Freitag
Vendredi
Vrijdag

4

Saturday
Samstag
Samedi
Zaterdag

5

Week	32	33	34	35	36
Mo·Mo·Lu·Ma	7	14	21	28	4
Tu·Di·Ma·Di	8	15	22	29	5
We·Mi·Me·Wo	9	16	23	30	6
Th·Do·Je·Do	10	17	24	31	7
Fr·Fr·Ve·Vr	11	18	25	1	8
Sa·Sa·Sa·Za	12	19	26	2	9
Su·So·Di·Zo	13	20	27	3	10

6

Sunday
Sonntag
Dimanche
Zondag

Portrait of Adele Bloch-Bauer II | Bildnis Adele Bloch-Bauer II
Portrait d'Adele Bloch-Bauer II | Retrato de Adele Bloch-Bauer II
1912. Oil on canvas, 190 x 120 cm
Vienna, Österreichische Galerie im Belvedere

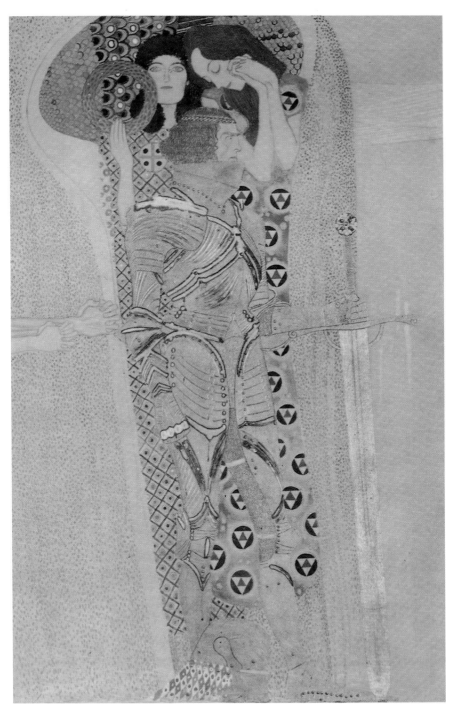

Beethoven Frieze, Yearning for Happiness (detail) | Beethovenfries, Die Sehnsucht nach dem Glück (Detail)
La frise Beethoven, L'Aspiration au bonheur (détail) | Friso Beethoven, El ansia de felicidad (detalle)
1902. Casein colours on stucco with semi-precious inlay and reed base, 220 x 2400 cm
Vienna, Österreichische Galerie im Belvedere / Photo: Archiv für Kunst und Geschichte, Berlin / Erich Lessing

August | August | Août | Augustus **2000**

Monday
Montag
Lundi
Maandag

7

UK Summer Bank Holiday (Scotland only)
IRL First Monday in August

Tuesday
Dienstag
Mardi
Dinsdag

8

Wednesday
Mittwoch
Mercredi
Woensdag

9

ZA National Women's Day

Thursday
Donnerstag
Jeudi
Donderdag

10

IL Tisha B'Av

Friday
Freitag
Vendredi
Vrijdag

11

Saturday
Samstag
Samedi
Zaterdag

12

Week	33	34	35	36	37
Mo·Mo·Lu·Ma	14	21	28	4	11
Tu·Di·Ma·Di	15	22	29	5	12
We·Mi·Me·Wo	16	23	30	6	13
Th·Do·Je·Do	17	24	31	7	14
Fr·Fr·Ve·Vr	18	25	1	8	15
Sa·Sa·Sa·Za	19	26	2	9	16
Su·So·Di·Zo	20	27	3	10	17

13

Sunday
Sonntag
Dimanche
Zondag

August | August | Août | Augustus **2000**

Monday Montag Lundi Maandag	**14**

Tuesday Dienstag Mardi Dinsdag	**15**

(F) Assomption
(D) Mariä Himmelfahrt (teilweise)
(A) Mariä Himmelfahrt
(B) Onze-Lieve-Vrouw-Hemelvaart | Assomption

Wednesday Mittwoch Mercredi Woensdag	**16**

Thursday Donnerstag Jeudi Donderdag	**17**

Friday Freitag Vendredi Vrijdag	**18**

Saturday Samstag Samedi Zaterdag	**19**

Week	34	35	36	37	38
Mo·Mo·Lu·Ma	21	28	4	11	18
Tu·Di·Ma·Di	22	29	5	12	19
We·Mi·Me·Wo	23	30	6	13	20
Th·Do·Je·Do	24	31	7	14	21
Fr·Fr·Ve·Vr	25	1	8	15	22
Sa·Sa·Sa·Za	26	2	9	16	23
Su·So·Di·Zo	27	3	10	17	24

20	Sunday Sonntag Dimanche Zondag

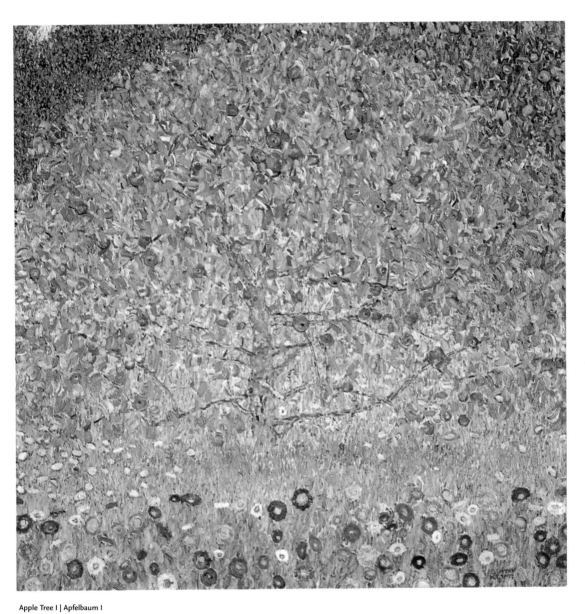

Apple Tree I | Apfelbaum I
Pommier I | Manzano I
c. 1912. Oil on canvas, 110 x 110 cm
Vienna, Österreichische Galerie im Belvedere / Photo: Archiv für Kunst und Geschichte, Berlin

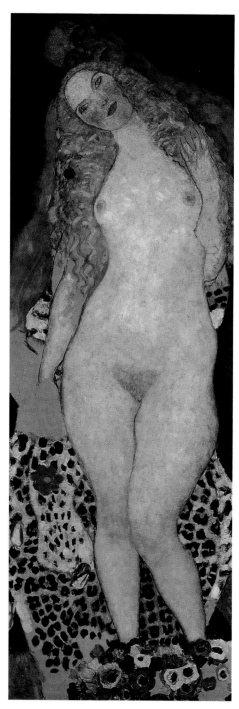

Adam and Eve (unfinished) | Adam und Eva (unvollendet)
Adam et Eve (inachevé) | Adán y Eva (inacabado)
1916/17. Oil on canvas, 173 x 60 cm
Vienna, Österreichische Galerie im Belvedere

August | August | Août | Augustus **2000**

Monday
Montag
Lundi
Maandag

21

Tuesday
Dienstag
Mardi
Dinsdag

22

Wednesday
Mittwoch
Mercredi
Woensdag

23

Thursday
Donnerstag
Jeudi
Donderdag

24

Friday
Freitag
Vendredi
Vrijdag

25

Saturday
Samstag
Samedi
Zaterdag

26

Week	35	36	37	38	39
Mo·Mo·Lu·Ma	28	4	11	18	25
Tu·Di·Ma·Di	29	5	12	19	26
We·Mi·Me·Wo	30	6	13	20	27
Th·Do·Je·Do	31	7	14	21	28
Fr·Fr·Ve·Vr	1	8	15	22	29
Sa·Sa·Sa·Za	2	9	16	23	30
Su·So·Di·Zo	3	10	17	24	1

27 Sunday
Sonntag
Dimanche
Zondag

August | August | Août | Augustus **2000**

Monday
Montag
Lundi
Maandag

28

UK Summer Bank Holiday (except Scotland)

Tuesday
Dienstag
Mardi
Dinsdag

29

Wednesday
Mittwoch
Mercredi
Woensdag

30

Thursday
Donnerstag
Jeudi
Donderdag

31

September | September | Septembre | September **2000**

Friday
Freitag
Vendredi
Vrijdag

1

Saturday
Samstag
Samedi
Zaterdag

2

Week	36	37	38	39	40
Mo·Mo·Lu·Ma	4	11	18	25	2
Tu·Di·Ma·Di	5	12	19	26	3
We·Mi·Me·Wo	6	13	20	27	4
Th·Do·Je·Do	7	14	21	28	5
Fr·Fr·Ve·Vr	8	15	22	29	6
Sa·Sa·Sa·Za	9	16	23	30	7
Su·So·Di·Zo	10	17	24	1	8

3

Sunday
Sonntag
Dimanche
Zondag

Unterach on the Attersee | Unterach am Attersee
Unterach sur l'Attersee | Unterach a orillas del Lago Atter
1915. Oil on canvas, 110 x 110 cm
Salzburg, Salzburger Landessammlungen-Rupertinum
Photo: Archiv für Kunst und Geschichte, Berlin / Erich Lessing

The Bride (unfinished) | Die Braut (unvollendet)
L'Epousée (inachevé) | La novia (inacabado)
1917/18. Oil on canvas, 166 x 190 cm
Private collection

September | September | Septembre | September **2000**

Monday
Montag
Lundi
Maandag

4

(USA) Labor Day
(CAN) Labour Day | Fête du Travail

Tuesday
Dienstag
Mardi
Dinsdag

5

Wednesday
Mittwoch
Mercredi
Woensdag

6

Thursday
Donnerstag
Jeudi
Donderdag

7

Friday
Freitag
Vendredi
Vrijdag

8

Saturday
Samstag
Samedi
Zaterdag

9

Week	37	38	39	40	41
Mo · Mo · Lu · Ma	11	18	25	2	9
Tu · Di · Ma · Di	12	19	26	3	10
We · Mi · Me · Wo	13	20	27	4	11
Th · Do · Je · Do	14	21	28	5	12
Fr · Fr · Ve · Vr	15	22	29	6	13
Sa · Sa · Sa · Za	16	23	30	7	14
Su · So · Di · Zo	17	24	1	8	15

10 Sunday
Sonntag
Dimanche
Zondag

September | September | Septembre | September **2000**

Monday
Montag
Lundi
Maandag

11

Tuesday
Dienstag
Mardi
Dinsdag

12

Wednesday
Mittwoch
Mercredi
Woensdag

13

Thursday
Donnerstag
Jeudi
Donderdag

14

Friday
Freitag
Vendredi
Vrijdag

15

⬭ Respect-for-the Aged Day

Saturday
Samstag
Samedi
Zaterdag

16

Week	38	39	40	41	42
Mo·Mo·Lu·Ma	18	25	2	9	16
Tu·Di·Ma·Di	19	26	3	10	17
We·Mi·Me·Wo	20	27	4	11	18
Th·Do·Je·Do	21	28	5	12	19
Fr·Fr·Ve·Vr	22	29	6	13	20
Sa·Sa·Sa·Za	23	30	7	14	21
Su·So·Di·Zo	24	1	8	15	22

17

Sunday
Sonntag
Dimanche
Zondag

The Dancer | Die Tänzerin
La Danseuse | La bailarina
c. 1916–1918. Oil on canvas, 180 x 90 cm
Private collection

Farmhouse in Upper Austria | Oberösterreichisches Bauernhaus
Ferme en Haute-Autriche | Casa de campo en la Alta Austria
1911/12. Oil on canvas, 110 x 110 cm
Vienna, Österreichische Galerie im Belvedere
Photo: Archiv für Kunst und Geschichte, Berlin

September | September | Septembre | September **2000**

Monday Montag Lundi Maandag	**18**
Tuesday Dienstag Mardi Dinsdag	**19**
Wednesday Mittwoch Mercredi Woensdag	**20**
Thursday Donnerstag Jeudi Donderdag	**21**
Friday Freitag Vendredi Vrijdag	**22**
Saturday Samstag Samedi Zaterdag	**23** (J) Autumn Equinox Day

Week	39	40	41	42	43
Mo·Mo·Lu·Ma	25	2	9	16	23
Tu·Di·Ma·Di	26	3	10	17	24
We·Mi·Me·Wo	27	4	11	18	25
Th·Do·Je·Do	28	5	12	19	26
Fr·Fr·Ve·Vr	29	6	13	20	27
Sa·Sa·Sa·Za	30	7	14	21	28
Su·So·Di·Zo	1	8	15	22	29

24 Sunday
Sonntag
Dimanche
Zondag   (ZA) Heritage Day

September | September | Septembre | September **2000**

Monday Montag Lundi Maandag	**25**	(ZA) Public Holiday
Tuesday Dienstag Mardi Dinsdag	**26**	
Wednesday Mittwoch Mercredi Woensdag	**27**	
Thursday Donnerstag Jeudi Donderdag	**28**	
Friday Freitag Vendredi Vrijdag	**29**	
Saturday Samstag Samedi Zaterdag	**30**	(IL) Rosh Hashanah

October | Oktober | Octobre | Oktober **2000**

Week	40	41	42	43	44
Mo·Mo·Lu·Ma	2	9	16	23	30
Tu·Di·Ma·Di	3	10	17	24	31
We·Mi·Me·Wo	4	11	18	25	1
Th·Do·Je·Do	5	12	19	26	2
Fr·Fr·Ve·Vr	6	13	20	27	3
Sa·Sa·Sa·Za	7	14	21	28	4
Su·So·Di·Zo	8	15	22	29	5

1 Sunday
Sonntag
Dimanche
Zondag

Portrait of Johanna Staude (unfinished) | Bildnis Johanna Staude (unvollendet)
Portrait de Johanna Staude (inachevé) | Retrato de Johanna Staude (inacabado)
1917/18. Oil on canvas, 70 x 50 cm
Vienna, Österreichische Galerie im Belvedere

Woman's Head | Frauenkopf
Tête de femme | Cabeza femenina
1918. Oil on canvas, 128 x 128 cm
Linz, Neue Galerie der Stadt Linz, Wolfgang-Gurlitt-Museum / Photo: Artothek, Peissenberg

Monday
Montag
Lundi
Maandag

2

Tuesday
Dienstag
Mardi
Dinsdag

3

Ⓓ Tag der Deutschen Einheit

Wednesday
Mittwoch
Mercredi
Woensdag

4

Thursday
Donnerstag
Jeudi
Donderdag

5

Friday
Freitag
Vendredi
Vrijdag

6

Saturday
Samstag
Samedi
Zaterdag

7

Week	41	42	43	44	45
Mo·Mo·Lu·Ma	9	16	23	30	6
Tu·Di·Ma·Di	10	17	24	31	7
We·Mi·Me·Wo	11	18	25	1	8
Th·Do·Je·Do	12	19	26	2	9
Fr·Fr·Ve·Vr	13	20	27	3	10
Sa·Sa·Sa·Za	14	21	28	4	11
Su·So·Di·Zo	15	22	29	5	12

8

Sunday
Sonntag
Dimanche
Zondag

October | Oktober | Octobre | Oktober **2000**

Monday
Montag
Lundi
Maandag

9

USA Columbus Day
CAN Thanksgiving Day | Action de Grâces
J Health-Sports Day
IL Yom Kippur

Tuesday
Dienstag
Mardi
Dinsdag

10

Wednesday
Mittwoch
Mercredi
Woensdag

11

Thursday
Donnerstag
Jeudi
Donderdag

12

Friday
Freitag
Vendredi
Vrijdag

13

Saturday
Samstag
Samedi
Zaterdag

14

IL Succoth

Week	42	43	44	45	46
Mo·Mo·Lu·Ma	16	23	30	6	13
Tu·Di·Ma·Di	17	24	31	7	14
We·Mi·Me·Wo	18	25	1	8	15
Th·Do·Je·Do	19	26	2	9	16
Fr·Fr·Ve·Vr	20	27	3	10	17
Sa·Sa·Sa·Za	21	28	4	11	18
Su·So·Di·Zo	22	29	5	12	19

15

Sunday
Sonntag
Dimanche
Zondag

Josef Hoffmann, Stoclet Palace, Brussels (Dining room, mosaics designed by Klimt) | Josef Hoffmann, Palais Stoclet, Brüssel (Speisesaal mit Mosaiken nach Klimt)
Josef Hoffmann, Palais Stoclet, Bruxelles (Salle à manger, mosaïque d'après Klimt) | Josef Hoffmann, Palacio Stoclet, Bruselas (Comedor con mosaicos según Klimt)
1905–1911. *Österreichische NationalBibliothek / © Photo: Bildarchiv / ÖNB, Wien*

Tree of Life (Working design for Stoclet Frieze, centre) | Lebensbaum (Werkvorlage zum Stoclet-Fries, mittlerer Teil)
L'Arbre de vie (projet d'œuvre pour la frise Stoclet, partie centrale) | Árbol de la vida (modelo para el Friso Stoclet, parte central)
c. 1905–1909. Tempera, watercolour, gold paint, silver-bronze, crayon, pencil, opaque white, gold leaf and silver leaf on paper, 195 x 102 cm
Vienna, Österreichisches Museum für Angewandte Kunst

October | Oktober | Octobre | Oktober **2000**

Monday
Montag
Lundi
Maandag

16

Tuesday
Dienstag
Mardi
Dinsdag

17

Wednesday
Mittwoch
Mercredi
Woensdag

18

Thursday
Donnerstag
Jeudi
Donderdag

19

Friday
Freitag
Vendredi
Vrijdag

20

Saturday
Samstag
Samedi
Zaterdag

21

IL Sh'mini Atz.

Week	43	44	45	46	47
Mo·Mo·Lu·Ma	23	30	6	13	20
Tu·Di·Ma·Di	24	31	7	14	21
We·Mi·Me·Wo	25	1	8	15	22
Th·Do·Je·Do	26	2	9	16	23
Fr·Fr·Ve·Vr	27	3	10	17	24
Sa·Sa·Sa·Za	28	4	11	18	25
Su·So·Di·Zo	29	5	12	19	26

22

Sunday
Sonntag
Dimanche
Zondag

IL Simchat Torah

October | Oktober | Octobre | Oktober **2000**

Monday
Montag
Lundi
Maandag

23

(NZ) Labour Day

Tuesday
Dienstag
Mardi
Dinsdag

24

Wednesday
Mittwoch
Mercredi
Woensdag

25

Thursday
Donnerstag
Jeudi
Donderdag

26

(A) Nationalfeiertag

Friday
Freitag
Vendredi
Vrijdag

27

Saturday
Samstag
Samedi
Zaterdag

28

Week	44	45	46	47	48
Mo·Mo·Lu·Ma	30	6	13	20	27
Tu·Di·Ma·Di	31	7	14	21	28
We·Mi·Me·Wo	1	8	15	22	29
Th·Do·Je·Do	2	9	16	23	30
Fr·Fr·Ve·Vr	3	10	17	24	1
Sa·Sa·Sa·Za	4	11	18	25	2
Su·So·Di·Zo	5	12	19	26	3

29 Sunday
Sonntag
Dimanche
Zondag

Portrait of Adele Bloch-Bauer I | Bildnis Adele Bloch-Bauer I
Portrait d'Adele Bloch-Bauer I | Retrato de Adele Bloch-Bauer I
1907. Oil and gold on canvas, 138 x 138 cm
Vienna, Österreichische Galerie im Belvedere
Photo: Artothek, Peissenberg

Portrait of Eugenia Primavesi | Bildnis Eugenia Primavesi
Portrait d'Eugénie Primavesi | Retrato de Eugenia Primavesi
c. 1913/14. Oil on canvas, 140 x 84 cm
Private collection

October | Oktober | Octobre | Oktober **2000**

Monday Montag Lundi Maandag	**30**	(IRL) Last Monday in October
Tuesday Dienstag Mardi Dinsdag	**31**	(D) Reformationstag (teilweise)

November | November | Novembre | November **2000**

Wednesday Mittwoch Mercredi Woensdag	**1**	(F) Toussaint (D) Allerheiligen (teilweise) (A) Allerheiligen (B) Allerheiligen | Toussaint
Thursday Donnerstag Jeudi Donderdag	**2**	(B) Allerzielen | Jour des Morts
Friday Freitag Vendredi Vrijdag	**3**	(J) Culture Day
Saturday Samstag Samedi Zaterdag	**4**	

Week	45	46	47	48	49
Mo · Mo · Lu · Ma	6	13	20	27	4
Tu · Di · Ma · Di	7	14	21	28	5
We · Mi · Me · Wo	8	15	22	29	6
Th · Do · Je · Do	9	16	23	30	7
Fr · Fr · Ve · Vr	10	17	24	1	8
Sa · Sa · Sa · Za	11	18	25	2	9
Su · So · Di · Zo	12	19	26	3	10

5 Sunday
Sonntag
Dimanche
Zondag

November | November | Novembre | November **2000**

Monday
Montag
Lundi
Maandag

6

Tuesday
Dienstag
Mardi
Dinsdag

7

Wednesday
Mittwoch
Mercredi
Woensdag

8

Thursday
Donnerstag
Jeudi
Donderdag

9

Friday
Freitag
Vendredi
Vrijdag

10

USA Public Holiday

Saturday
Samstag
Samedi
Zaterdag

11

USA Veterans' Day
CAN Remembrance Day | Jour du Souvenir
F Armistice 1918
B Wapenstilstand | Armistice

Week	46	47	48	49	50
Mo·Mo·Lu·Ma	13	20	27	4	11
Tu·Di·Ma·Di	14	21	28	5	12
We·Mi·Me·Wo	15	22	29	6	13
Th·Do·Je·Do	16	23	30	7	14
Fr·Fr·Ve·Vr	17	24	1	8	15
Sa·Sa·Sa·Za	18	25	2	9	16
Su·So·Di·Zo	19	26	3	10	17

12 Sunday
Sonntag
Dimanche
Zondag

The Tall Poplars II (Approaching Thunderstorm) | Die große Pappel II (Aufsteigendes Gewitter)
Le Grand Peuplier II (Avant l'orage) | El gran álamo II (se levanta tormenta)
1903. Oil on canvas, 100 x 100 cm
Vienna, Dr. Rudolf Leopold Collection
Photo: Archiv für Kunst und Geschichte, Berlin

Portrait of Margaret Stonborough-Wittgenstein | Bildnis Margaret Stonborough-Wittgenstein
Portrait de Margaret Stonborough-Wittgenstein | Retrato de Margaret Stonborough-Wittgenstein
1905. Oil on canvas, 180 x 90.5 cm
Munich, Bayerische Staatsgemäldesammlungen / Photo: Artothek, Peissenberg

Monday
Montag
Lundi
Maandag

13

Tuesday
Dienstag
Mardi
Dinsdag

14

Wednesday
Mittwoch
Mercredi
Woensdag

15

Thursday
Donnerstag
Jeudi
Donderdag

16

Friday
Freitag
Vendredi
Vrijdag

17

Saturday
Samstag
Samedi
Zaterdag

18

Week	47	48	49	50	51
Mo · Mo · Lu · Ma	20	27	4	11	18
Tu · Di · Ma · Di	21	28	5	12	19
We · Mi · Me · Wo	22	29	6	13	20
Th · Do · Je · Do	23	30	7	14	21
Fr · Fr · Ve · Vr	24	1	8	15	22
Sa · Sa · Sa · Za	25	2	9	16	23
Su · So · Di · Zo	26	3	10	17	24

19 Sunday
Sonntag
Dimanche
Zondag

November | November | Novembre | November **2000**

Monday
Montag
Lundi
Maandag

20

Tuesday
Dienstag
Mardi
Dinsdag

21

Wednesday
Mittwoch
Mercredi
Woensdag

22

Ⓓ Buß- und Bettag (teilweise)

Thursday
Donnerstag
Jeudi
Donderdag

23

Ⓤ︎ Thanksgiving Day
Ⓙ Labor-Thanksgiving Day

Friday
Freitag
Vendredi
Vrijdag

24

Saturday
Samstag
Samedi
Zaterdag

25

Week	48	49	50	51	52
Mo·Mo·Lu·Ma	27	4	11	18	25
Tu·Di·Ma·Di	28	5	12	19	26
We·Mi·Me·Wo	29	6	13	20	27
Th·Do·Je·Do	30	7	14	21	28
Fr·Fr·Ve·Vr	1	8	15	22	29
Sa·Sa·Sa·Za	2	9	16	23	30
Su·So·Di·Zo	3	10	17	24	31

26 Sunday
Sonntag
Dimanche
Zondag

The Kiss (detail) | Der Kuß (Detail)
Le Baiser (détail) | El beso (detalle)
1907/08. Oil on canvas, 180 x 180 cm
Vienna, Österreichische Galerie im Belvedere

Death and Life | Tod und Leben
La Vie et la Mort | Muerte y vida
1916. Oil on canvas, 178 x 198 cm
Vienna, Dr. Rudolf Leopold Collection

November | November | Novembre | November **2000**

Monday
Montag
Lundi
Maandag

27

Tuesday
Dienstag
Mardi
Dinsdag

28

Wednesday
Mittwoch
Mercredi
Woensdag

29

Thursday
Donnerstag
Jeudi
Donderdag

30

December | Dezember | Décembre | December **2000**

Friday
Freitag
Vendredi
Vrijdag

1

Saturday
Samstag
Samedi
Zaterdag

2

Week	49	50	51	52	1
Mo·Mo·Lu·Ma	4	11	18	25	1
Tu·Di·Ma·Di	5	12	19	26	2
We·Mi·Me·Wo	6	13	20	27	3
Th·Do·Je·Do	7	14	21	28	4
Fr·Fr·Ve·Vr	8	15	22	29	5
Sa·Sa·Sa·Za	9	16	23	30	6
Su·So·Di·Zo	10	17	24	31	7

3

Sunday
Sonntag
Dimanche
Zondag

December | Dezember | Décembre | December **2000**

Monday
Montag
Lundi
Maandag

4

Tuesday
Dienstag
Mardi
Dinsdag

5

Wednesday
Mittwoch
Mercredi
Woensdag

6

Thursday
Donnerstag
Jeudi
Donderdag

7

Friday
Freitag
Vendredi
Vrijdag

8

Ⓐ Mariä Empfängnis

Saturday
Samstag
Samedi
Zaterdag

9

Week	50	51	52	1	2
Mo·Mo·Lu·Ma	11	18	25	1	8
Tu·Di·Ma·Di	12	19	26	2	9
We·Mi·Me·Wo	13	20	27	3	10
Th·Do·Je·Do	14	21	28	4	11
Fr·Fr·Ve·Vr	15	22	29	5	12
Sa·Sa·Sa·Za	16	23	30	6	13
Su·So·Di·Zo	17	24	31	7	14

10 Sunday
Sonntag
Dimanche
Zondag

Nymphs (Silver Fish) | Nixen (Silberfische)
Ondines (Poissons d'argent) | Ondinas (Peces plateados)
c. 1899. Oil on canvas, 82 x 52 cm
Vienna, Zentralsparkasse der Gemeinde Wien

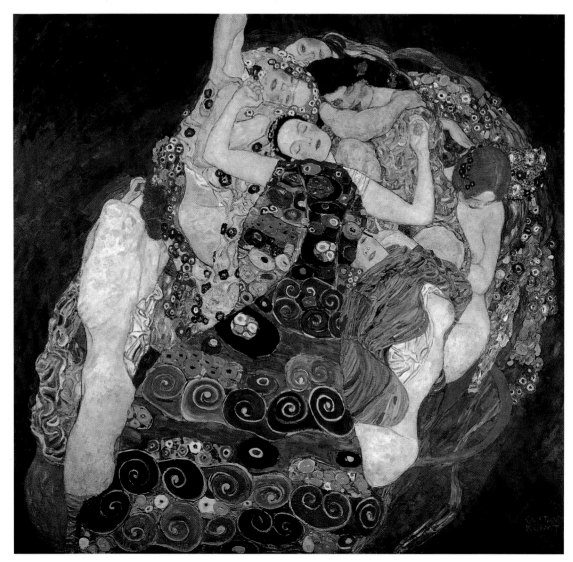

The Virgin | Die Jungfrau
La Jeune Fille | La virgen
1913. Oil on canvas, 190 x 200 cm
Prague, Národni Galerie

December | Dezember | Décembre | December **2000**

Monday
Montag
Lundi
Maandag

11

Tuesday
Dienstag
Mardi
Dinsdag

12

Wednesday
Mittwoch
Mercredi
Woensdag

13

Thursday
Donnerstag
Jeudi
Donderdag

14

Friday
Freitag
Vendredi
Vrijdag

15

Saturday
Samstag
Samedi
Zaterdag

16

ZA Day of Reconciliation

Week	51	52	1	2	3
Mo·Mo·Lu·Ma	18	25	1	8	15
Tu·Di·Ma·Di	19	26	2	9	16
We·Mi·Me·Wo	20	27	3	10	17
Th·Do·Je·Do	21	28	4	11	18
Fr·Fr·Ve·Vr	22	29	5	12	19
Sa·Sa·Sa·Za	23	30	6	13	20
Su·So·Di·Zo	24	31	7	14	21

17

Sunday
Sonntag
Dimanche
Zondag

December | Dezember | Décembre | December **2000**

Monday
Montag
Lundi
Maandag

18

Tuesday
Dienstag
Mardi
Dinsdag

19

Wednesday
Mittwoch
Mercredi
Woensdag

20

Thursday
Donnerstag
Jeudi
Donderdag

21

Friday
Freitag
Vendredi
Vrijdag

22

(IL) Hanukkah

Saturday
Samstag
Samedi
Zaterdag

23

(J) Emperor's Birthday

Week		52	1	2	3	4
Mo·Mo·Lu·Ma		25	1	8	15	22
Tu·Di·Ma·Di		26	2	9	16	23
We·Mi·Me·Wo		27	3	10	17	24
Th·Do·Je·Do		28	4	11	18	25
Fr·Fr·Ve·Vr		29	5	12	19	26
Sa·Sa·Sa·Za		30	6	13	20	27
Su·So·Di·Zo		31	7	14	21	28

24

Sunday
Sonntag
Dimanche
Zondag

Pallas Athene | Pallas Athene
Pallas Athéna | Palas Atenea
1898. Oil on canvas, 75 x 75 cm
Vienna, Historisches Museum der Stadt Wien / Photo: Archiv für Kunst und Geschichte, Berlin / Erich Lessing

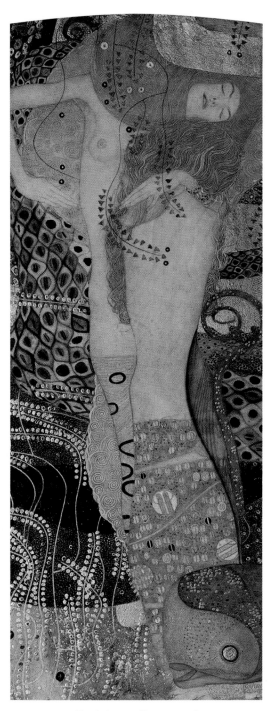

Water Serpents I (Girlfriends) | Wasserschlangen I (Freundinnen)
Serpents d'eau I (Les Amies) | Serpientes acuáticas I (Amigas)
1904–1907. Gold and watercolours on parchment, 50 x 20 cm
Vienna, Österreichische Galerie im Belvedere

December | Dezember | Décembre | December **2000**

Monday
Montag
Lundi
Maandag

25

Christmas Day | Noël | 1. Weihnachtstag |
Christtag | 1° Kerstdag | Kerstmis | Natale

Tuesday
Dienstag
Mardi
Dinsdag

26

(UK) (IRL) (NZ) (AUS) (ZA) (D) (A)
(CH) (NL) (B)
Boxing Day | Saint Stephen's Day | Day of
Goodwill | 2. Weihnachtstag | Stephanitag |
Stefanstag | 2° Kerstdag | Tweede Kerstdag |
Lendemain de Noël | S. Stefano

Wednesday
Mittwoch
Mercredi
Woensdag

27

Thursday
Donnerstag
Jeudi
Donderdag

28

Friday
Freitag
Vendredi
Vrijdag

29

Saturday
Samstag
Samedı
Zaterdag

30

Week	1	2	3	4	5
Mo·Mo·Lu·Ma	1	8	15	22	29
Tu·Di·Ma·Di	2	9	16	23	30
We·Mi·Me·Wo	3	10	17	24	31
Th·Do·Je·Do	4	11	18	25	1
Fr·Fr·Ve·Vr	5	12	19	26	2
Sa·Sa·Sa·Za	6	13	20	27	3
Su·So·Di·Zo	7	14	21	28	4

31

Sunday
Sonntag
Dimanche
Zondag

Public Holidays 2000 | Feiertage 2000 | Jours fériés pour 2000 | Días festivos en 2000

Österreich (A)
1.1 Neujahr
6.1 Heilige Drei Könige
23.4 Ostersonntag
24.4 Ostermontag
1.5 Tag der Arbeit
1.6 Christi Himmelfahrt
11.6 Pfingstsonntag
12.6 Pfingstmontag
22.6 Fronleichnam
15.8 Mariä Himmelfahrt
26.10 Nationalfeiertag
1.11 Allerheiligen
8.12 Mariä Empfängnis
25.12 Christfest
26.12 Stephanitag

Australia (AUS)
1.1 New Year's Day
26.1 Australia Day
21.4 Good Friday
23.4 Easter Sunday
24.4 Easter Monday
25.4 Anzac Day
25.12 Christmas Day
26.12 Boxing Day

Belgique | België (B)
1.1 Nouvel An | Nieuwjaar
23.4 Pâques | Pasen
24.4 Lundi de Pâques |
Paasmaandag
1.5 Fête du Travail |
Feest van de Arbeid
1.6 Ascension | Onze-Lieve-
Heer-Hemelvaart
11.6 Pentecôte | Pinksteren
12.6 Lundi de Pentecôte |
Pinkstermaandag
21.7 Fête Nationale |
Nationale Feestdag
15.8 Assomption | Onze-Lieve-
Vrouw-Hemelvaart
1.11 Toussaint | Allerheiligen
2.11 Jour des Morts | Allerzielen
11.11 Armistice | Wapenstilstand
25.12 Noël | Kerstmis
26.12 Lendemain de Noël |
Tweede Kerstdag

Brasil (BR)
1.1 Ano Novo
7.3 Carnaval
21.4 Sexta-feira da Paixão
21.4 Tiradentes
1.5 Dia do Trabalho
22.6 Corpus Christi
7.9 Independência do Brasil
12.10 Nossa Senhora Aparecida

2.11 Finados
15.11 Proclamação da República
25.12 Natal

Catalunya (C)
1.1 Any Nou
6.1 Epifania
21.4 Divendres Sant
23.4 Diumenge de Pascua
24.4 Dilluns de Pascua
1.5 Festa del Treball
24.6 Sant Joan
15.8 L'Assumpció
11.9 Diada Nacional de
Catalunya
12.10 Festa de la Hispanitat
1.11 Tots Sants
8.12 La Immaculada
25.12 Nadal
26.12 Sant Esteve

Canada (CDN)
1.1 New Year's Day |
Jour de l'An
21.4 Good Friday | Vendredi
Saint
23.4 Easter Sunday | Pâques
22.5 Victoria Day | Fête de la
Reine et de Dollard
24.6 Québec's National Holiday |
Fête Nationale du Québec
1.7 Canada Day | Jour de la
Confédération
4.9 Labour Day | Fête du
Travail
9.10 Thanksgiving Day |
Action de Grâces
11.11 Remembrance Day |
Jour du Souvenir
25.12 Christmas Day | Noël

Schweiz | Suisse | Svizzera (CH)
1.1 Neujahr | Nouvel An |
Capo d'Anno
21.4 Karfreitag | Vendredi Saint |
Venerdì Santo
23.4 Ostern | Pâques | Pasqua
24.4 Ostermontag | Lundi
de Pâques | Lunedì
dell'Angelo
1.6 Auffahrt | Ascension |
Ascensione
11.6 Pfingstsonntag |
Pentecôte | Pentecoste
12.6 Pfingstmontag |
Lundi de Pentecôte |
Lunedì di Pentecoste
1.8 Bundesfeiertag | Fête na-
tionale suisse | Festa na-
zionale svizzera

25.12 Weihnachten | Noël |
Natale
26.12 Stefanstag | S. Etienne |
S. Stefano

Colombia (CO)
1.1 Año Nuevo
10.1 Reyes Magos
20.3 San José
20.4 Jueves Santo
21.4 Viernes Santo
1.5 Día del Trabajo
5.6 Ascención del Señor
11.6 Sagrado Corazón
26.6 Corpus Christi
3.7 San Pedro y San Pablo
20.7 Día de la Independencia
7.8 Batalla de Boyacá
21.8 Asunción de la Virgen
16.10 Día de la Raza
6.11 Día de todos los Santos
13.11 Independencia de
Cartagena
8.12 Inmaculada Concepción
25.12 Navidad

Bundesrepublik Deutschland (D)
1.1 Neujahr
6.1 Heilige Drei Könige
(teilweise)
21.4 Karfreitag
23.4 Ostersonntag
24.4 Ostermontag
1.5 Maifeiertag
1.6 Christi Himmelfahrt
11.6 Pfingstsonntag
12.6 Pfingstmontag
22.6 Fronleichnam (teilweise)
15.8 Mariä Himmelfahrt
(teilweise)
3.10 Tag der Deutschen Einheit
31.10 Reformationstag
(teilweise)
1.11 Allerheiligen (teilweise)
22.11 Buß- und Bettag
(teilweise)
25.12 1. Weihnachtstag
26.12 2. Weihnachtstag

Danmark (DK)
1.1 Nytår
16.4 Dronning Margrethe II's
fødselsdag
20.4 Skærtorsdag
21.4 Langfredag
23.4 Påske
24.4 Påske
19.5 St. Bededag
1.6 Kristi Himmelfartsdag

5.6 Grundlovsdag
11.6 Pinse
12.6 Pinse
25.12 Jul
26.12 Jul

España (E)
1.1 Año Nuevo
6.1 Epifanía del Señor
21.4 Viernes Santo
23.4 Pascua
1.5 Fiesta del Trabajo
15.8 Asunción de la Virgen
12.10 Fiesta Nacional
1.11 Todos los Santos
6.12 Día de la Constitución
8.12 Inmaculada Concepción
25.12 Natividad del Señor

France (F)
1.1 Jour de l'An
23.4 Pâques
24.4 Lundi de Pâques
1.5 Fête du Travail
8.5 Fête de la Libération
1.6 Ascension
11.6 Pentecôte
12.6 Lundi de Pentecôte
14.7 Fête Nationale
15.8 Assomption
1.11 Toussaint
11.11 Armistice 1918
25.12 Noël

Italia (I)
1.1 Capodanno
6.1 Epifania
23.4 Pasqua
24.4 Lunedì di Pasqua
25.4 Anniversario della
Liberazione
1.5 Festa del Lavoro
15.8 Ascensione di Maria Vergine
1.11 Tutti i Santi
8.12 Immacolata Concezione
25.12 Natale
26.12 S. Stefano

Israel (IL)
22.1 Tu B'Shevat
21.3 Purim
20.4 Passover
2.5 Yom Hashoah
10.5 Yom Haatzmaut
9.6 Shavuot
10.8 Tisha B'Av
30.9 Rosh Hashanah
9.10 Yom Kippur
14.10 Succoth

21.10	Sh'mini Atz.
22.10	Simchat Torah
22.12	Hanukkah

(IRL)
Ireland
1.1	New Year's Day
3.1.	Public Holiday
17.3	Saint Patrick's Day
23.4	Easter Sunday
24.4	Easter Monday
1.5	First Monday in May
5.6	First Monday in June
7.8	First Monday in August
30.10	Last Monday in October
25.12	Christmas Day
26.12	Saint Stephen's Day

(J)
Japan
1.1	New Year's Day
10.1	Coming-of-Age Day
11.2	Commemoration of the Founding of the Nation
20.3	Vernal Equinox Day
29.4	Greenery Day
3.5	Constitution Day
4.5	Public Holiday
5.5	Children's Day
20.7	Marine Day
15.9	Respect-for-the-Aged Day
23.9	Autumn Equinox Day
9.10	Health-Sports Day
3.11	Culture Day
23.11	Labor-Thanksgiving Day
23.12	Emperor's Birthday

(L)
Luxembourg | Leitzeburg | Luxemburg
1.1	Jour de l'An	Neijoodschdag	Neujahr
23.4	Pâques	Ouschter-sonndeg	Ostersonntag
24.4	Lundi de Pâques	Ouschter-méindeg	Ostermontag
1.5	Fête du Travail	Eischte Mee	Maifeiertag
1.6	Ascension	Christi-Himmelfaart	Christi Himmelfahrt
11.6	Pentecôte	Péngscht-sonndeg	Pfingstsonntag
12.6	Lundi de Pentecôte	Péngschtméindeg	Pfingstmontag
23.6	Fête Nationale	National-feierdag	Nationalfeiertag
15.8	Assomption	Léiffrakrautdag	Mariä Himmelfahrt
1.11	Toussaint	Allerhelgen	Allerheiligen
25.12	Noël	Krëschtdag	Weihnachten
26.12	Lendemain de Noël	Stiewesdag	2. Weihnachtstag

(MEX)
México
1.1	Año Nuevo
5.2	Aniversario de la Constitución
21.3	Natalicio de Benito Juárez
20.4	Jueves Santo
21.4	Viernes Santo
1.5	Día del Trabajo
16.9	Día de la Independencia
20.11	Aniversario de la Revolución Mexicana
25.12	Navidad

(N)
Norge
1.1	Nyttårsdag
16.4	Palmesøndag
20.4	Skjærtorsdag
21.4	Langfredag
23.4	1. påskedag
24.4	2. påskedag
1.5	Offentlig høytidsdag
17.5	Grunnlovsdag
1.6	Kristi himmelfartsdag
11.6	1. pinsedag
12.6	2. pinsedag
25.12	1. juledag
26.12	2. juledag

(NL)
Nederland
1.1	Nieuwjaarsdag
21.4	Goede Vrijdag
23.4	1e Paasdag
24.4	2e Paasdag
30.4	Koninginnedag
1.6	Hemelvaartsdag
11.6	1e Pinksterdag
12.6	2e Pinksterdag
25.12	1e Kerstdag
26.12	2e Kerstdag

(NZ)
New Zealand
1.1	New Year's Day
3.1	Public Holiday
4.1	Public Holiday
6.2	Waitangi Day
21.4	Good Friday
23.4	Easter Sunday
24.4	Easter Monday
25.4	Anzac Day
5.6	Queen's Birthday
23.10	Labour Day
25.12	Christmas Day
26.12	Boxing Day

(P)
Portugal
1.1	Ano Novo
21.4	Sexta-feira Santa
23.4	Domingo de Páscoa
25.4	Dia da Liberdade
1.5	Dia do Trabalho
10.6	Dia Nacional
22.6	Corpo de Deus
15.8	Assunção de Nossa Senhora
5.10	Implantação da República
1.11	Todos os Santos
1.12	Dia da Restauração
8.12	Imaculada Conceição
25.12	Dia de Natal

(RA)
Argentina
1.1	Año Nuevo
20.4	Jueves Santo
21.4	Viernes Santo
1.5	Día del Trabajador
25.5	Fundación del Primer Gobierno Nacional
10.6	Recuperación de las Islas Malvinas
20.6	Día de la Bandera
9.7	Día de la Independencia
17.8	Muerte del General San Martín
12.10	Descubrimiento de América
8.12	Inmaculada Concepción de la Virgen María
25.12	Navidad

(RCH)
Chile
1.1	Año Nuevo
21.4	Viernes Santo
22.4	Sábado Santo
23.4	Pascua de Resurrección
1.5	Día del Trabajo
21.5	Combate Naval de Iquique
11.6	Corpus Christi
15.8	Asunción de la Virgen
18.9	Fiestas Patrias
19.9	Día del Ejército
12.10	Día de la Hispanidad
1.11	Todos los Santos
8.12	Immaculada Concepción
25.12	Navidad

(S)
Sverige
1.1	Nyårsdagen
6.1	Trettondedag Jul
21.4	Långfredagen
23.4	Påskdagen
24.4	Annandag Påsk
1.5	Första Maj
1.6	Kristi Himmelsfärds dag
11.6	Pingstdagen
12.6	Annandag Pingst
24.6	Midsommardagen
4.11	Alla Helgons dag
25.12	Juldagen
26.12	Annandag Jul

(UK)
United Kingdom
1.1	New Year's Day
3.1	Public Holiday
17.3	Saint Patrick's Day (Northern Ireland only)
21.4	Good Friday
23.4	Easter Sunday
24.4	Easter Monday (except Scotland)
1.5	May Bank Holiday
29.5	Spring Bank Holiday
7.8	Summer Bank Holiday (Scotland only)
28.8	Summer Bank Holiday (except Scotland)
25.12	Christmas Day
26.12	Boxing Day

(USA)
United States
1.1	New Year's Day
17.1	Martin Luther King Day
21.2	Presidents' Day
23.4	Easter Sunday
29.5	Memorial Day
4.7	Independence Day
4.9	Labor Day
9.10	Columbus Day
10.11	Public Holiday
11.11	Veterans' Day
23.11	Thanksgiving Day
25.12	Christmas Day

(ZA)
South Africa
1.1	New Year's Day
21.3	Human Rights Day
21.4	Good Friday
24.4	Family Day
27.4	Constitution Day
1.5	Workers' Day
16.6	Youth Day
9.8	National Women's Day
24.9	Heritage Day
25.9	Public Holiday
16.12	Day of Reconciliation
25.12	Christmas Day
26.12	Day of Goodwill

Some international holidays may be subject to change.

Year Planner | Jahresplaner | Planning | Planning **2001**

January			February			March			April		
1	Mo	1	1	Th		1	Th		1	Su	
2	Tu		2	Fr		2	Fr		2	Mo	14
3	We		3	Sa		3	Sa		3	Tu	
4	Th		4	Su		4	Su		4	We	
5	Fr		5	Mo	6	5	Mo	10	5	Th	
6	Sa		6	Tu		6	Tu		6	Fr	
7	Su		7	We		7	We		7	Sa	
8	Mo	2	8	Th		8	Th		8	Su	
9	Tu		9	Fr		9	Fr		9	Mo	15
10	We		10	Sa		10	Sa		10	Tu	
11	Th		11	Su		11	Su		11	We	
12	Fr		12	Mo	7	12	Mo	11	12	Th	
13	Sa		13	Tu		13	Tu		13	Fr	
14	Su		14	We		14	We		14	Sa	
15	Mo	3	15	Th		15	Th		15	Su	
16	Tu		16	Fr		16	Fr		16	Mo	16
17	We		17	Sa		17	Sa		17	Tu	
18	Th		18	Su		18	Su		18	We	
19	Fr		19	Mo	8	19	Mo	12	19	Th	
20	Sa		20	Tu		20	Tu		20	Fr	
21	Su		21	We		21	We		21	Sa	
22	Mo	4	22	Th		22	Th		22	Su	
23	Tu		23	Fr		23	Fr		23	Mo	17
24	We		24	Sa		24	Sa		24	Tu	
25	Th		25	Su		25	Su		25	We	
26	Fr		26	Mo	9	26	Mo	13	26	Th	
27	Sa		27	Tu		27	Tu		27	Fr	
28	Su		28	We		28	We		28	Sa	
29	Mo	5				29	Th		29	Su	
30	Tu					30	Fr		30	Mo	18
31	We					31	Sa				

Year Planner | Jahresplaner | Planning | Planning **2001**

May		June		July		August	
1 Tu		1 Fr		1 Su		1 We	
2 We		2 Sa		2 Mo	27	2 Th	
3 Th		3 Su		3 Tu		3 Fr	
4 Fr		4 Mo	23	4 We		4 Sa	
5 Sa		5 Tu		5 Th		5 Su	
6 Su		6 We		6 Fr		6 Mo	32
7 Mo	19	7 Th		7 Sa		7 Tu	
8 Tu		8 Fr		8 Su		8 We	
9 We		9 Sa		9 Mo	28	9 Th	
10 Th		10 Su		10 Tu		10 Fr	
11 Fr		11 Mo	24	11 We		11 Sa	
12 Sa		12 Tu		12 Th		12 Su	
13 Su		13 We		13 Fr		13 Mo	33
14 Mo	20	14 Th		14 Sa		14 Tu	
15 Tu		15 Fr		15 Su		15 We	
16 We		16 Sa		16 Mo	29	16 Th	
17 Th		17 Su		17 Tu		17 Fr	
18 Fr		18 Mo	25	18 We		18 Sa	
19 Sa		19 Tu		19 Th		19 Su	
20 Su		20 We		20 Fr		20 Mo	34
21 Mo	21	21 Th		21 Sa		21 Tu	
22 Tu		22 Fr		22 Su		22 We	
23 We		23 Sa		23 Mo	30	23 Th	
24 Th		24 Su		24 Tu		24 Fr	
25 Fr		25 Mo	26	25 We		25 Sa	
26 Sa		26 Tu		26 Th		26 Su	
27 Su		27 We		27 Fr		27 Mo	35
28 Mo	22	28 Th		28 Sa		28 Tu	
29 Tu		29 Fr		29 Su		29 We	
30 We		30 Sa		30 Mo	31	30 Th	
31 Th				31 Tu		31 Fr	

Year Planner | Jahresplaner | Planning | Planning 2001

September		October		November		December	
1 Sa		1 Mo	40	1 Th		1 Sa	
2 Su		2 Tu		2 Fr		2 Su	
3 Mo	36	3 We		3 Sa		3 Mo	49
4 Tu		4 Th		4 Su		4 Tu	
5 We		5 Fr		5 Mo	45	5 We	
6 Th		6 Sa		6 Tu		6 Th	
7 Fr		7 Su		7 We		7 Fr	
8 Sa		8 Mo	41	8 Th		8 Sa	
9 Su		9 Tu		9 Fr		9 Su	
10 Mo	37	10 We		10 Sa		10 Mo	50
11 Tu		11 Th		11 Su		11 Tu	
12 We		12 Fr		12 Mo	46	12 We	
13 Th		13 Sa		13 Tu		13 Th	
14 Fr		14 Su		14 We		14 Fr	
15 Sa		15 Mo	42	15 Th		15 Sa	
16 Su		16 Tu		16 Fr		16 Su	
17 Mo	38	17 We		17 Sa		17 Mo	51
18 Tu		18 Th		18 Su		18 Tu	
19 We		19 Fr		19 Mo	47	19 We	
20 Th		20 Sa		20 Tu		20 Th	
21 Fr		21 Su		21 We		21 Fr	
22 Sa		22 Mo	43	22 Th		22 Sa	
23 Su		23 Tu		23 Fr		23 Su	
24 Mo	39	24 We		24 Sa		24 Mo	52
25 Tu		25 Th		25 Su		25 Tu	
26 We		26 Fr		26 Mo	48	26 We	
27 Th		27 Sa		27 Tu		27 Th	
28 Fr		28 Su		28 We		28 Fr	
29 Sa		29 Mo	44	29 Th		29 Sa	
30 Su		30 Tu		30 Fr		30 Su	
		31 We				31 Mo	1

Addresses, Notes | Adressen, Notizen | Adresses, Notes | Adressen, Notities